P9-EMM-953

# SECRET HISTORY

# PROCOPIVS

# SECRET HISTORY

*Translated by Richard Atwater*

Dorset Press
*New York*

This edition published by Dorset Press,
a division of Marboro Books Corp.
Offset by permission of the University of Michigan Press.

1992 Dorset Press

ISBN 1-56619-048-9

Printed and bound in the United States of America

M 9 8 7 6 5 4 3 2 1

# CONTENTS

# SECRET
# HISTORY

## BY THE
## HISTORIAN

In what I have written on the Roman wars up to the present point, the story was arranged in chronological order and as completely as the times then permitted. What I shall write now follows a different plan, supplementing the previous formal chronicle with a disclosure of what really happened throughout the Roman Empire. You see, it was not possible, during the life of certain persons, to write the truth of what they did, as a historian should. If I had, their hordes of spies would have found out about it, and they would have put me to a most horrible death. I could not even trust my nearest relatives. That is why I was compelled to hide the real explanation of many matters glossed over in my previous books.

These secrets it is now my duty to tell and reveal the remaining hidden matters and motives. Yet when I approach this different task, I find it hard indeed to have to stammer and retract what I have written before about the lives of Justinian and Theodora. Worse yet, it occurs to me that what I am now about to tell will seem neither probable nor plausible to future generations, especially as time flows on and my story becomes ancient history. I fear they may think me a writer of fiction, and even put me among the poets.

However, I have this much to cheer me, that my account will not be unendorsed by other testimony: so I shall not shrink from the duty of completing this work.

For the men of today, who know best the truth of these matters, will be trustworthy witnesses to posterity of the accuracy of my evidence.

Still another thing for a long time deferred my passion to relieve myself of this untold tale. For I wondered if it might be prejudicial to future generations, and the wickedness of these deeds had not best remain unknown to later times: lest future tyrants, hearing, might emulate them. It is deplorably natural that most monarchs mimic the sins of their predecessors and are most readily disposed to turn to the evils of the past.

But, finally, I was again constrained to proceed with this history, for the reason that future tyrants may see also that those who thus err cannot avoid retribution in the end, since the persons of whom I write suffered that judgment. Furthermore, the disclosure of these actions and tempers will be published for all time, and in consequence others will perhaps feel less urge to transgress.

For who now would know of the unchastened life of Semiramis or the madness of Sardanapalus or Nero, if the record had not thus been written by men of their own times? Besides, even those who suffer similarly from later tyrants will not find this narrative quite unprofitable. For the miserable find comfort in the philosophy that not on them alone has evil fallen.

Accordingly, I begin the tale. First I shall reveal the folly of Belisarius, and then the depravity of Justinian and Theodora.

## I. HOW THE GREAT GENERAL BELISARIUS WAS HOODWINKED BY HIS WIFE

The father of Belisarius's wife, a lady whom I have mentioned in my former books, was (and so was her grandfather) a charioteer, exhibiting that trade in Constantinople and Thessalonica. Her mother was one of the wenches of the theater; and she herself from the first led an utterly wanton life. Acquainted with magic drugs used by her parents before her, she learned how to use those of compelling qualities and became the wedded wife of Belisarius, after having already borne many children.

Now she was unfaithful as a wife from the start, but was careful to conceal her indiscretions by the usual precautions; not from any awe of her spouse (for she never felt any shame at anything, and fooled him easily with her deceptions), but because she feared the punishment of the Empress. For Theodora hated her, and had already shown her teeth. But when that Queen became involved in difficulties, she won her friendship by helping her, first to destroy Silverius, as shall be related presently, and later to ruin John of Cappadocia, as I have told elsewhere. After that, she became more and more fearless, and casting all concealment aside, abandoned herself to the winds of desire.

There was a youth from Thrace in the house of Belisarius: Theodosius by name, and of the Eunomian heresy by descent. On the eve of his expedition to Libya, Belisarius baptized this boy in holy water and received him in his arms as a member henceforth of the family, welcoming him with his wife as their son, according to the Christian rite of adoption. And Antonina not only embraced Theodosius with reasonable fondness as her son by holy word, and thus cared for him, but soon, while her husband was away on his campaign, became wildly in love with him; and, out of her senses with this malady, shook off all fear and shame of God and man. She began by enjoying him surreptitiously, and ended by dallying with him in the presence of the men servants and waiting maids. For she was now possessed by passion and, openly overwhelmed with love, could see no hindrance to its consummation.

Once, in Carthage, Belisarius caught her in the very act, but allowed himself to be deceived by his wife. Finding the two in an underground room, he was very angry; but she said, showing no fear or attempt to keep anything hidden, "I came here with the boy to bury the most precious part of our plunder, where the Emperor will not discover it." So she said by way of excuse, and he dismissed the matter as if he believed her, even as he saw Theodosius's trousers belt somewhat unmodestly unfastened. For so bound by love for the woman was he, that he preferred to distrust the evidence of his own eyes.

As her folly progressed to an indescribable extent, those who saw what was going on kept silent, except one slave, Macedonia by name. When Belisarius was in Syracuse as the conqueror of Sicily, she made her master swear solemnly never to betray her to her mistress, and then told him the whole story, presenting as witnesses two slave boys attending the bed-chamber.

When he heard this, Belisarius ordered one of his guards to put Theodosius away; but the latter learned of this in time to flee to Ephesus. For most of the servants, inspired by the weakness of the husband's character, were more anxious to please his wife than to show loyalty to him, and so betrayed the order he had given. But Constantine, when he saw Belisarius's grief at what had befallen him, sympathized entirely except to comment, "I would have tried to kill the woman rather than the young man." Antonina heard of this, and hated him in secret. How malicious was her spite against him shall be shown; for she was a scorpion who could hide her sting.

But not long after this, by the enchantment either of philtres or of her caresses, she persuaded her husband that the charges against her were untrue. Without more ado he sent word to Theodosius to return, and promised to turn Macedonia and the two slave boys over to his wife. She first cruelly cut out their tongues, it is said, and then cut their bodies into little bits which were put into sacks and thrown into the sea. One of her slaves, Eugenius, who had already wrought the outrage on Silverius, helped her in this crime.

And it was not long after this that Belisarius was persuaded by his wife to kill Constantine. What happened at that time concerning Presidius and the daggers I have narrated in my previous books. For while Belisarius would have preferred to let Constantine alone, Antonina gave him no peace until his remark, which

I have just repeated, was avenged. And as a result of this murder, much enmity was aroused against Belisarius in the hearts of the Emperor and all the most important of the Romans.

So matters progressed. But Theodosius said he was unable to return to Italy, where Belisarius and Antonina were now staying, unless Photius were put out of the way. For this Photius was the sort who would bite if anyone got the better of him in anything, and he had reason to be choked with indignation at Theodosius. Though he was the rightful son, he was utterly disregarded while the other grew in power and riches: they say that from the two palaces at Carthage and Ravenna Theodosius had taken plunder amounting to a hundred centenaries, as he alone had been given the management of these conquered properties.

But Antonina, when she learned of Theodosius's fear, never ceased laying snares for her son and planning deadly plots against his welfare, until he saw he would have to escape to Constantinople if he wished to live. Then Theodosius came to Italy and her. There they stayed in the satisfaction of their love, unhindered by the complaisant husband; and later she took them both to Constantinople. There Theodosius became so worried lest the affair became generally known, that he was at his wit's end. He saw it would be impossible to fool everybody, as the woman was no longer able to conceal her passion and indulge it secretly, but thought nothing of being in fact and in reputation an avowed adulteress.

Therefore he went back to Ephesus, and having his head shaved after the religious custom, became a monk.

Whereupon Antonina, insane over her loss, exhibited her grief by donning mourning; and went around the house shrieking and wailing, lamenting even in the presence of her husband what a good friend she had lost, how faithful, how tender, how loving, how energetic! In the end, even her spouse was won over to join in her sorrow. And so the poor wretch wept too, calling for his beloved Theodosius. Later he even went to the Emperor and implored both him and the Empress, till they consented to summon Theodosius to return, as one who was and would always be a necessity in the house of Belisarius.

But Theodosius refused to leave his monastery, saying he was completely resolved to give himself forever to the cloistered life. This noble pronouncement, however, was not entirely sincere, for he was aware that as soon as Belisarius left Constantinople, it would be possible for him to come secretly to Antonina. Which, indeed, he did.

## II. HOW BELATED JEALOUSY AFFECTED BELISARIUS'S MILITARY JUDGMENT

For soon Belisarius went off to war on Chosroes, and he took Photius with him; but Antonina remained behind, though this was contrary to her usual habit. She had always preferred to voyage wherever her husband went, lest he, being alone, come to his senses and, forgetting her enchantments, think of her for once as she deserved. But now, so that Theodosius might have free access to her, she planned once more how to rid herself permanently of Photius. She bribed some of Belisarius's guards to slander and insult her son at all times; while she, writing letters almost every day, denounced him, and thus set everything in motion against him. Compelled by all of this to counterplot against his mother, Photius got a witness to come from Constantinople with evidence of Theodosius's commerce with Antonina, took him to Belisarius, and commanded him to tell the whole story.

When Belisarius heard it, he became passionately angry, fell at Photius's feet, kissed them, and begged him to revenge one who had been so wronged by those who should least have treated him thus. "My dearest boy," he said, "your father, whoever he was, you have never known, for he left you at your mother's breast when the sands of his life were measured. Nor have you

even benefited from his estate, since he was not over-
blessed with wealth. But brought up by me, though I
was only your stepfather, you have arrived at an age
where it becomes you to avenge my wrongs. I, who
have raised you to consular rank, and given you the
opportunity of acquiring such riches, might call myself
your father and mother and entire kindred, and I
would be right, my son. For it is not by their kinship
of blood, but by their friendly deeds that men are wont
to measure their bonds to one another.

"Now the hour has come, when you must not only
look on me in the ruin of my household and the loss
of my greatest treasure, but as one sharing the shame of
your mother in the reproach of all mankind. And consider too, that the sins of women injure not only their
husbands, but touch even more bitterly their children,
whose reputation suffers the greater from this reason,
that they are expected to inherit the disposition of those
who bore them.

"Yet remember this of me, that I still love my wife
exceedingly well; and if it is in my power to punish
the ruiner of my house, to her I shall do no hurt. But
while Theodosius is present, I cannot condone this
charge against her."

When he had heard this, Photius agreed to serve
him in everything; but at the same time he was afraid
lest some trouble might come to himself from it, for
he had little confidence in Belisarius's strength of will,
where his wife was concerned. And among other un-
happy possibilities, he remembered with distaste what
had happened to Macedonia. So he had Belisarius exchange with him all the oaths that are held most sacred

and binding among Christians, and each swore never to betray the other, even in the most mortal peril.

Now for the present they decided the time had not yet come to take action. But as soon as Antonina should arrive from Constantinople and Theodosius return to Ephesus, Photius was to go to Ephesus and dispose without difficulty of Theodosius and his property.

It was at this time that they had invaded the Persian country with the entire army, and there occurred to John of Cappadocia what is reported in my previous works. There I had to hush up one matter out of prudence, namely, that it was not without malice aforethought that Antonina deceived John and his daughter, but by many oaths, than which none is more reverenced by the Christians, she induced them to trust her as one who would never use them ill. After she had done this, feeling more confident than before of the friendship of the Empress, she sent Theodosius to Ephesus, and herself, with no suspicion of opposition, set out for the East.

Belisarius had just taken the fort of Sisauranum when the news of her coming was brought to him; and he, setting everything else as nothing in comparison, ordered the army to retire. It so happened, as I have shown elsewhere, that other things had occurred to the expedition which fitted in with his order to withdraw. However, as I said in the foreword to this book, it was not safe for me at that time to tell all the underlying motives of these events.

Accusation was consequently made against Belisarius by all the Romans that he had put the most urgent affairs of state below the lesser interests of his personal household. For the fact was that, possessed with jealous passion for his wife, he was unwilling to go far away from Roman territory, so that as soon as he should learn his wife was coming from Constantinople, he could immediately seize her and avenge himself on Theodosius.

For this reason he ordered the forces under Arethas to cross the Tigris River; and they returned home, having accomplished nothing worthy of mention. And he himself was careful not to leave the Roman frontier for much more than a one hour's ride. Indeed, the fort of Sisauranum, going by way of the city of Nisibis, is not more than a day's journey for a well-mounted man from the Roman border; and by another route is only half that distance. Yet if he had been willing in the beginning to cross the Tigris with his entire army, I believe he could have taken all the plunder in the land of Assyria, and marched as far as the city of Ctesiphon, with none to hinder him. And he could have rescued the captured Antiochans and whatever other Romans misfortune had brought there, and restored them to their native lands.

Furthermore, he was culpable for Chosroes's unhindered return home from Colchis. How this happened I shall now reveal. When Chosroes, Cabades's son, invading the land of Colchis, accomplished not only what I have elsewhere narrated, but captured Petra, a great part of the army of the Medes was destroyed, either in battle or because of the difficulty of the country. For Lazica, as I have explained, is almost roadless and very mountainous. Also pestilence, falling upon them, had destroyed most of the army, and many had died from lack of necessary food and treatment. It was at this time that messengers came from Persia with news that Belisarius, having conquered Nabedes in battle before the city of Nisibis, was approaching; that he had taken the fort of Sisauranum by siege, captured at the point of the spear Bleschames and eight hundred Persian cavalry; and that he had sent a second army of Romans under Arethas, ruler of the Saracens, to cross the Tigris and ravage all the land there that heretofore had not known fear.

It happened also that the army of Huns which Chosroes had sent into Roman Armenia, to create a diversion there so that the Romans would not notice his expedition into Lazica, had fallen into the hands of Valerian and his Romans, as other messengers now reported; and that these barbarians had been badly beaten in battle, and most of them killed. When the Persians heard this, already in low spirits over their ill fortune among the Lazi, they now feared if they should meet a hostile army in their present difficulties, among precipices and wilderness, they would all perish in disorder. And they feared, too, for their children and their wives and their country; indeed, the noblest men in the army of the Medes reviled Chosroes, calling him one who had broken his plighted word and the common law of man, by invading in time of peace the land of the Romans. He had wronged, they cried, the oldest and greatest of all nations, which he could not possibly surpass in war. A mutiny was imminent.

Aroused at this, Chosroes found the following remedy for the trouble. He read them a letter which the

Empress had recently written to Zaberganes. This was the letter:

"How highly I esteem you, Zaberganes, and that I believe you friendly to our State, you, who were ambassador to us not so long ago, are well aware. Would you not be acting suitably to this high opinion which I have for you, if you could persuade King Chosroes to choose peace with our government? If you do this, I can promise you will be rewarded by my husband, who does nothing without my advice."

Chosroes read this aloud, and asked the Persian leaders if they thought this was an Empire which a woman managed. Thus he calmed their nervousness. But even so, he withdrew from the place with considerable anxiety, thinking that at any moment Belisarius's forces would confront him. And when none of the enemy appeared to bar his retreat, with great relief he marched back to his native land.

## III. SHOWING THE DANGER OF INTERFERING WITH A WOMAN'S INTRIGUES

On his return to Roman territory, Belisarius found his wife just arriving from Constantinople. He put her under guard in disgrace, and often was on the point of putting her to death; but each time he weakened, overcome, I suppose, by the rekindling of his love for her. But they say he was also driven from his senses by magic philtres she gave him.

Meanwhile the outraged Photius had gone to Ephesus, taking the eunuch Calligonus, pander for his mistress, with him, in chains; and under the whip, during the course of his journey Calligonus confessed all his lady's secrets. But Theodosius again learned of his peril, and fled to the Church of St. John the Apostle, which is the holiest and most revered sanctuary thereabouts. However, Andrew, Bishop of Ephesus, was bribed by Photius to give the man up into his hands.

Theodora was now in some fear for Antonina, for she had heard what had happened to her; so she sent word to Belisarius to bring his wife to Constantinople. Photius, hearing of this, sent Theodosius to Cilicia, where his own lancers and shield-bearers happened to be wintering; enjoining upon those who took him thither to do so as secretly as possible, and on arriving in Cilicia to hide him privately in the garrison, letting no one know where in the world he was. Then, with Calligonus and Theodosius's considerable moneys, Photius went to Constantinople.

Now the Empress gave evidence to all mankind that for every murder to which she was indebted, she could pay in greater and even more savage requital. For Antonina had betrayed for her one enemy, when she had lately ensnared the Cappadocian; but she ruined, for Antonina's sake, a number of blameless men. Some of Belisarius's and Photius's acquaintances she put to the torture, when the only charge against them was that they were friends of the two (and to this day we do not know what was their ultimate fate), and others she banished into exile on the same accusation.

One man who had accompanied Photius to Ephesus, a Senator who was also named Theodosius, not only lost his property but was thrown into a dungeon, where he was fastened to a manger by a rope around his neck so short that the noose was always tight and could not be slackened. Consequently the poor man had to stand at the manger all the time, whether he ate or sought sleep or performed the other needs of the body. The only difference between him and an ass, was that he could not bray. The time the man passed in this condition was not less than four months; after which, overcome by melancholy, he went mad, and as such they set him free to die.

The reluctant Belisarius she forced to become reconciled with his wife; while Photius, after she had him tortured like a slave and scourged on the back and shoulders, was ordered to tell where Theodosius and the pander were. But in spite of his anguish at the torture he kept silent as he had sworn to do; though he had always been delicate and sickly, had had to be very careful of his health, and was hitherto inexperienced in such outrage and ill treatment. Yet none of Belisarius's secrets did he divulge.

Later, however, everything that up to this time had been concealed came to light. Discovering Calligonus in the neighborhood, Theodora handed him over to Antonina, and then had Theodosius brought back to Constantinople, where she hid him in her palace. On the day after his arrival she sent for Antonina. "My dearest lady," she said, "a pearl fell into my hands yesterday, such a one as no mortal has ever seen. If you wish, I will not grudge you a sight of this jewel, but will show it to you." Not knowing what had happened, her friend begged Theodora to show her the pearl; and the Empress, leading Theodosius from the rooms of one of the eunuchs, revealed him.

For a moment Antonina, speechless with joy, remained dumb. Then she broke into an ecstasy of gratitude, and called Theodora her saviour, her benefactress, and her true mistress. Thereafter, the Empress kept Theodosius in the palace, wrapping him in every luxury, and declared she would even make him general of all the Roman forces before long. Justice, however, intervened. Carried off by a dysentery, he disappeared from the world of men.

Now in Theodora's palace were certain secret dungeon rooms: dark, unknown, and remote, wherein there was no difference between day and night. In one of these Photius languished for a long time. He had the good fortune, however, to escape, not once, but twice. The first time he took refuge in the Church of the Virgin Mother, which is the most holy and famous of the churches in Constantinople, and there took his place at the sacred table as a suppliant. But she captured him even here, and had him removed by force. The second time he fled to the Church of St. Sophia and sought sanctuary at the holy font, which of all places the Christians most reverence. Yet even from here the woman was able to drag him: for to her no spot was too awful or venerable to transgress, and she thought nothing of violating all the sanctuaries put together. Like all the rest of the people, the Christian priests were struck dumb with horror, but stood to one side and suffered her to do as she willed.

Now for three years Photius remained thus in his cell; and then the prophet Zechariah came to him in a dream, and ordered him in the name of the Lord to escape, promising to aid him in this. Trusting in the vision, he broke loose again, and unnoticed by anyone made his way to Jerusalem. Though he passed through countless thousands of men on his flight, not one of them saw the youth. There he shaved his head, assumed the garb of the monks, and was free at last from the punishment of Theodora.

But Belisarius, disregarding his word of honor, took no measures to avenge his accomplice's suffering of such impious treatment as has been told. And all of his military expeditions from this time on failed, presumably by the will of God. For his next campaign against Chosroes and the Medes, who were for the third time invading Roman territory, was severely criticized; though one good thing was said of him, that he had

driven the foe back. But when Chosroes crossed the
Euphrates River, took the great city of Callinicus without a battle, and enslaved myriads of Roman citizens,
while Belisarius was careful not even to pursue the
enemy when he retired, he won the reputation of being
one of two things—either a traitor or a coward.

## IV. HOW THEODORA HUMILIATED THE CONQUEROR OF AFRICA AND ITALY

Soon after this, a further disaster befell him. The
plague, which I have described elsewhere, became epi-
demic at Constantinople, and the Emperor Justinian
was taken grievously ill; it was even said he had died
of it. Rumor spread this report till it reached the Roman
army camp. There some of the officers said that if the
Romans tried to establish anyone else at Constantinople
as Emperor, they would never recognize him. Presently,
the Emperor's health bettered, and the officers of the
army brought charges against each other, the generals
Peter and John the Glutton alleging they had heard
Belisarius and Buzes making the above declaration.

This hypothetical mutiny the indignant Queen took
as intended by the two men to refer to herself. So she
recalled all the officers to Constantinople to investigate
the matter; and she summoned Buzes impromptu to
her private quarters, on the pretext she wished to discuss with him matters of sudden urgency.

Now underneath the palace was an underground cellar, secure and labyrinthian, comparable to the infernal regions, in which most of those who gave offense to her were eventually entombed. And so Buzes was thrown into this oubliette, and there the man, though of consular rank, remained with no one cognizant of his fate. Neither, as he sat there in darkness, could he ever know whether it was day or night, nor could he learn from anyone else; for the man who each day threw him his food was dumb, and the scene was that of one wild beast confronting another. Everybody soon thought him dead, but no one dared to mention even his memory. But after two years and four months, Theodora took pity on the man and released him. Ever after he was half blind and sick in body. This is what she did to Buzes.

Belisarius, although none of the charges against him were proved, was at the insistence of the Empress relieved of his command by the Emperor; who appointed Martinus in his place as General of the armies of the East. Belisarius's lancers and shield-bearers, and such of his servants as were of military use, he ordered to be divided between the other generals and certain of the palace eunuchs. Drawing lots for these men and their arms, they portioned them as the chances fell. And his friends, and all who formerly had served him, were forbidden ever to visit Belisarius. It was a bitter sight, and one no one would ever have thought credible, to see Belisarius a private citizen in Constantinople, almost deserted, melancholy and miserable of countenance, and ever expectant of a further conspiracy to accomplish his death.

Then the Empress learned he had acquired great wealth in the East, and sent one of the eunuchs of the palace to confiscate it. Antonina, as I have told, was now quite out of temper with her husband, but on the most friendly and intimate terms with the Queen, since she had got rid of John of Cappadocia. So, to please Antonina, Theodora arranged everything so that the wife would appear to have asked mercy for her husband, and from such peril to have saved his life; and the poor wretch not only became quite reconciled to her, but let her make him her humblest slave for having saved him from the Queen. And this is how that happened.

One morning, Belisarius went to the palace as usual with his few and pitiful followers. Finding the Emperor and Empress hostile, he was further insulted in their presence by baseborn and common men. Late in the evening he went home, often turning around as he withdrew and looking in every direction for those who might be advancing to put him to death. Accompanied by this dread, he entered his home and sat down alone upon his couch. His spirit broken, he failed even to remember the time when he was a man; sweating, dizzy and trembling, he counted himself lost; devoured by slavish fears and mortal worry, he was completely emasculated.

Antonina, who neither knew just what arrangement of his fate had been made nor much cared what would become of him, was walking up and down nearby pretending a heartburn; for they were not exactly on friendly terms. Meanwhile, an officer of the palace, Quadratus by name, had come as the sun went down, and passing through the outer hall, suddenly stood at the door of the men's apartments to say he had been sent here by the Empress. And when Belisarius heard that, he drew up his arms and legs onto the couch and lay down on his back, ready for the end. So far had all manhood left him.

Quadratus, however, approached only to hand him a letter from the Queen. And thus the letter read: "You know, Sir, your offense against us. But because I am greatly indebted to your wife, I have decided to dismiss all charges against you and give her your life. So for the future you may be of good cheer as to your personal safety and that of your property; but we shall know by what happens to you how you conduct yourself toward her."

When Belisarius read this, intoxicated with joy and yearning to give evidence of his gratitude, he leapt from his couch and prostrated himself at the feet of his wife. With each hand fondling one of her legs, licking with his tongue the sole of first one of her feet and then the other, he cried that she was the cause of his life and of his safety: henceforth he would be her faithful slave, instead of her lord and master.

The Empress then gave thirty gold centenaries of his property to the Emperor, and returned what was left to Belisarius. This is what happened to the great general to whom destiny had not long before given both Gelimer and Vitiges to be captives of his spear! But the wealth that this subject of theirs had acquired had long ago gnawed jealous wounds in the hearts of Justinian and Theodora, who deemed it grown too big for any but the imperial coffers. And they said he had concealed most of Gelimer's and Vitiges's moneys, which by conquest belonged to the State, and had handed over only a small fraction, hardly worth accepting by an Emperor. Yet, when they counted the labors the man had accomplished, and the cries of reproach they might arouse among the people, since they had no credible pretext for punishing him, they kept their peace: until now, when the Empress, discovering him out of his senses with terror, at one fell stroke managed to become mistress of all his fortune.

To tie him further to her, she betrothed Joannina, Belisarius's only daughter, to Anastasius her nephew.

Belisarius now asked to be given back his old command, and as General of the East lead the Roman armies once more against Chosroes and the Medes; but Antonina would not hear of it. It was there she had been insulted by him before, she said, and she never wanted to see the place again. Accordingly, Belisarius was instead made Count of the imperial remounts, and fared forth a second time to Italy; agreeing with the Emperor, they say, not to ask him at any time for money toward this war, but to prepare all the military equipment from his private purse.

Now everybody took it for granted that Belisarius had arranged this with his wife and made the agreement about the expedition with the Emperor, merely so as to get away from his humiliating position in Constantinople; and that as soon as he had gotten outside the city, he intended to take up arms and retaliate, nobly and as becomes a man, against his wife and those who had done him wrong. Instead, he made light of all he had experienced, forgot or discounted his word of honor to Photius and his other friends, and followed his wife about in a perfect ecstasy of love: and that when she had now arrived at the age of sixty years.

However, as soon as he arrived in Italy, some new and different trouble happened with each fresh day, for even Providence had turned against him. For the plans this General had laid in the former campaign against Theodatus and Vitiges, though they did not seem to be fitting to the event, usually turned out to his advantage; while now, though he was credited with laying better plans, as was to be expected after his previous experience in warfare, they all turned out badly: so that the final judgment was that he had no sense of strategy.

Indeed, it is not by the plans of men, but by the hand of God that the affairs of men are directed; and this men call Fate, not knowing the reason for what things they see occur; and what seems to be without cause is easy to call the accident of chance. Still, this is a matter every mortal will decide for himself according to his taste.

## V. HOW THEODORA
## TRICKED THE
## GENERAL'S DAUGHTER

From his second expedition to Italy Belisarius brought
back nothing but disgrace: for in the entire five years
of the campaign he was unable to set foot on that land,
as I have related in my former books, because there
was no tenable position there; but all this time sailed up
and down along the coast.

Totila, indeed, was willing enough to meet him before his city walls, but could not catch him there, since
like the rest of the Roman army he was afraid to fight.
Wherefore Belisarius recovered nothing of what had
been lost, but even lost Rome in addition; and everything else, if there were anything left to lose. His mind
was filled with avarice during this time, and he thought
of nothing but base gain. Since he had been given no
funds by the Emperor, he plundered nearly all the
Italians living in Ravenna and Sicily, and wherever
else he found opportunity: collecting a bill, as it were,
for which those who dwelt there were in no way responsible. Thus, he even went to Herodian and asked
him for money, and his threats so enraged Herodian
that he rebelled against the Roman army and gave his
services, with those of his followers and the city of
Spoletum, to Totila and the Goths.

And now I shall show how it came about that Belisarius and John, the nephew of Vitalian, became

estranged: a division that brought great disaster to Roman affairs.

Now so thoroughly did the Empress hate Germanus, and so conspicuously, that no one dared to become a relative of his, though he was the nephew of the Emperor. His sons remained unmarried while she lived, and his daughter Justina, though in the flower of eighteen summers, was still unwedded. Consequently, when John, sent by Belisarius, arrived in Constantinople, Germanus was forced to approach him as a possible son-in-law, though John was not at all worthy in station of such an alliance. But when they had come to an agreement, they bound each other by most solemn oaths to complete the alliance by all means in their power; and this was necessary because neither had any confidence in the good faith of the other. For John knew he was seeking a marriage far above his rank, and Germanus feared that even this man might try to slip out of the contract.

The Empress, of course, was unable to contain herself at this: and in every way, by every possible device, however unworthy, tried to hinder the event. When, for all her menaces, she was unable to deter either of them, she publicly threatened to put John to death. After this, on John's return to Italy, fearing Antonina might join the plot against him, he did not dare to meet Belisarius until she left for Constantinople. That Antonina had been charged by the Queen to help murder him, no one could have thought unlikely; and when he considered Antonina's habits and Belisarius's enslavement by his wife, John was as greatly as he was reasonably alarmed.

The Roman expedition, already on its last legs, now collapsed entirely. And this is how Belisarius concluded the Gothic war. In despair he begged the Emperor to let him come home as fast as he could sail. And when he received the monarch's permission to do this, he left straightway in high spirits, bidding a long farewell to the Roman army and to Italy. He left almost everything in the power of the enemy; and while he was on his way home, Perusia, hard pressed by a most bitter siege, was captured and submitted to every possible misery, as I have elsewhere related.

As if this were not enough, he suffered a further personal misfortune in the following manner. The Empress Theodora, desiring to marry the daughter of Belisarius to her nephew, worried the girl's parents with frequent letters. To avoid this alliance, they delayed the ceremony "until they could both be present at it," and then, when the Empress summoned them to Constantinople, pretended they were unable at the time to leave Italy. But the Queen was still determined her nephew should be master of Belisarius's wealth, for she knew his daughter would inherit it, as Belisarius had no other child. Yet she had no confidence in Antonina; and fearing that after her own life was ended, Antonina would not be loyal to her house, for all that she had been so helpful in the Empress's emergencies, and that she would break the agreement, Theodora did an unholy thing.

She made the boy and girl live together without any ceremony. And they say she forced the girl against her will to submit to his clandestine embrace, so that, being thus deflowered, the girl would agree to the marriage, and the Emperor could not forbid the event. However, after the first ravishing, Anastasius and the girl fell warmly in love with each other, and for not less than eight months continued their unmarital relations.

But when, after Theodora's death, Antonina came to Constantinople, she was unwilling to forget the outrage the Queen had committed against her. Not bothering about the fact that if she united her daughter to any other man, she would be making an ex-prostitute out of her, she refused to accept Theodora's nephew as a son-in-law, and by force tore the girl, ignoring her fondest pleadings, from the man she loved.

For this act of senseless obstinacy she was universally censured. Yet when her husband came home, she easily persuaded him to approve her course: which should have openly disclosed the character of the man. Still, though he had pledged himself to Photius and others of his friends, and then broken his word, there were plenty who sympathized with him. For they thought the reason for his perjury was not uxoriousness, but his fear of the Empress. But after Theodora died, as I have told, he still took no thought of Photius or any of his friends; and it was clear he called Antonina his mistress, and Calligonus the pander, his master. And then all men saw his shame, made him a public laughing stock, and reviled him to his face as a nitwit. Now was the folly of Belisarius completely revealed.

As for Sergius, son of Bacchus, and his misdeeds in Libya, I have described that affair sufficiently in my chapter elsewhere on the subject: how he was most guilty for the disaster there to Roman power, and how he disregarded the gospel oath he had sworn to the

Levathae, and criminally put to death their eighty
ambassadors. So there remains for me now to add only
this, that neither did these men come to Sergius with
any intention of treachery, nor did Sergius have any
suspicion that they did; but nevertheless, after inviting
them to a banquet under pledge of safety, he put them
shamefully to death. This resulted in the loss of Solomon, the Roman army, and all the Libyans. For consequent to this affair, especially after Solomon's death,
as I have told, neither officer nor soldier was willing
to venture the dangers of battle. Most notably John,
son of Sisinniolus, kept entirely from the field of war,
because of his hatred of Sergius, until Areobindus came
to Libya.

This Sergius was a luxurious person and no soldier;
juvenile in nature and in years; a jealous and swagger-
ing bully; a wanton liver and a blowhard. But after he
became the accepted suitor of her niece and was thus
related to Antonina, Belisarius's wife, the Empress
would not allow him to be punished or removed from
his command, even when she saw Libya sure to be lost.
And with the Emperor's consent she even let Solomon,
Sergius's brother, go scotfree after the murder of Pegasius. How this happened I shall now relate.

After Pegasius had ransomed Solomon from the
Levathae, and the barbarians had gone home, Solomon,
with Pegasius his ransomer and a few soldiers, set out
for Carthage. And on the way Pegasius reminded Solomon of the wrong he had done, and said he should
thank God for his rescue from the enemy. Solomon,
vexed at being reproached for having been taken cap-
tive, straightway slew Pegasius; and this was his re-

quital to the man who had saved him. But when Solomon arrived in Constantinople, the Emperor pardoned him for the crime on the ground that the man he killed was a traitor to the Roman state. So Solomon, thus escaping justice, left gladly for the East to visit his native country and his family. Yet God's vengeance overtook him on the very journey, and removed him from the world of men.

This is the explanation of the affair between Solomon and Pegasius.

## VI. IGNORANCE OF THE EMPEROR JUSTIN, AND HOW HIS NEPHEW JUSTINIAN WAS THE VIRTUAL RULER

I come now to the tale of what sort of beings Justinian and Theodora were, and how they brought confusion on the Roman state.

During the rule of Emperor Leo in Constantinople, three young farmers of Illyrian birth, named Zimarchus, Ditybistus, and Justin of Bederiana, after a desperate struggle with poverty, left their homes to try their fortune in the army. They made their way to Constantinople on foot, carrying on their shoulders their blankets in which were wrapped no other equipment except biscuits they had baked at home. When they arrived and were admitted into military service, the Emperor chose them for the palace guard; for they were all three fine-looking men.

Later, when Anastasius succeeded to the throne, war broke out with the Isaurians when that nation rebelled; and against them Anastasius sent a considerable army under John the Hunchback. This John for some offense threw Justin into the guardhouse, and on the following day would have sentenced him to death, had he not been stopped by a vision appearing to him in a dream. For in this dream, the general said, he beheld a being, gigantic in size and in every way mightier than mortals: and this being commanded him to release the man whom he had arrested that day. Waking from his sleep, John said, he decided the dream was not worth considering. But the next night the vision returned, and again he heard the same words he had heard before; yet even so he was not persuaded to obey its command. But for the third time the vision appeared in his dreams, and threatened him with fearful consequences if he did not do as the angel ordered: warning that he would be in sore need of this man and his family thereafter, when the day of wrath should overtake him. And this time Justin was released.

As time went on, this Justin came to great power. For the Emperor Anastasius appointed him Count of the palace guard; and when the Emperor departed from this world, by the force of his military power Justin seized the throne. By this time he was an old man on the verge of the grave, and so illiterate that he could neither read nor write: which never before could have been said of a Roman ruler. It was the custom for an Emperor to sign his edicts with his own hand, but he neither made decrees nor was able to understand the business of state at all.

The man on whom it befell to assist him as Quaestor was named Proclus; and he managed everything to suit himself. But so that he might have some evidence of the Emperor's hand, he invented the following device for his clerks to construct. Cutting out of a block of wood the shapes of the four letters required to make the Latin word, they dipped a pen into the ink used by emperors for their signatures, and put it in the Emperor's fingers. Laying the block of wood I have described on the paper to be signed, they guided the Emperor's hand so that his pen outlined the four letters, following all the curves of the stencil: and thus they withdrew with the FIAT of the Emperor. This is how the Romans were ruled under Justin.

His wife was named Lupicina: a slave and a barbarian, she was bought to be his concubine. With Justin, as the sun of his life was about to set, she ascended the throne.

Now Justin was able to do his subjects neither harm nor good. For he was simple, unable to carry on a conversation or make a speech, and utterly bucolic. His nephew Justinian, while still a youth, was the virtual ruler, and the cause of more and worse calamities to the Romans than any one man in all their previous history that has come down to us. For he had no scruples against murder or the seizing of other persons' property; and it was nothing to him to make away with myriads of men, even when they gave him no cause.

He had no care for preserving established customs, but was always eager for new experiments, and, in short, was the greatest corrupter of all noble traditions.

Though the plague, described in my former books, attacked the whole world, no fewer men escaped than perished of it; for some never were taken by the disease, and others recovered after it had smitten them. But this man, not one of all the Romans could escape; but as if he were a second pestilence sent from heaven, he fell on the nation and left no man quite untouched. For some he slew without reason, and some he released to struggle with penury, and their fate was worse than that of those who had perished, so that they prayed for death to free them from their misery; and others he robbed of their property and their lives together.

When there was nothing left to ruin in the Roman state, he determined the conquest of Libya and Italy, for no other reason than to destroy the people there, as he had those who were already his subjects.

Indeed, his power was not ten days old, before he slew Amantius, chief of the palace eunuchs, and several others, on no graver charge than that Amantius had made some rash remark about John, Archbishop of the city. After this, he was the most feared of men.

Immediately after this he sent for the rebel Vitalian, to whom he had first given pledges of safety, and partaken with him of the Christian communion. But soon after he became suspicious and jealous, and murdered Vitalian and his companions at a banquet in the palace: thus showing he considered himself in no way bound by the most sacred of pledges.

## VII. OUTRAGES OF THE
## BLUES

The people had since long previous time been divided, as I have explained elsewhere, into two factions, the Blues and the Greens. Justinian, by joining the former party, which had already shown favor to him, was able to bring everything into confusion and turmoil, and by its power to sink the Roman state to its knees before him. Not all the Blues were willing to follow his leadership, but there were plenty who were eager for civil war. Yet even these, as the trouble spread, seemed the most prudent of men, for their crimes were less awful than was in their power to commit. Nor did the Green partisans remain quiet, but showed their resentment as violently as they could, though one by one they were continually punished; which, indeed, urged them each time to further recklessness. For men who are wronged are likely to become desperate.

Then it was that Justinian, fanning the flame and openly inciting the Blues to fight, made the whole Roman Empire shake on its foundation, as if an earthquake or a cataclysm had stricken it, or every city within its confines had been taken by the foe. Everything everywhere was uprooted: nothing was left undisturbed by him. Law and order, throughout the State, overwhelmed by distraction, were turned upside down.

First the rebels revolutionized the style of wearing their hair. For they had it cut differently from the rest of the Romans: not molesting the mustache or beard, which they allowed to keep on growing as long as it would, as the Persians do, but clipping the hair short on the front of the head down to the temples, and letting it hang down in great length and disorder in the back, as the Massageti do. This weird combination they called the Hun haircut.

Next they decided to wear the purple stripe on their togas, and swaggered about in a dress indicating a rank above their station: for it was only by ill-gotten money they were able to buy this finery. And the sleeves of their tunics were cut tight about the wrists, while from there to the shoulders they were of an ineffable fullness; thus, whenever they moved their hands, as when applauding at the theater or encouraging a driver in the hippodrome, these immense sleeves fluttered conspicuously, displaying to the simple public what beautiful and well-developed physiques were these that required such large garments to cover them. They did not consider that by the exaggeration of this dress the meagerness of their stunted bodies appeared all the more noticeable. Their cloaks, trousers, and boots were also different: and these too were called the Hun style, which they imitated.

Almost all of them carried steel openly from the first, while by day they concealed their two-edged daggers along the thigh under their cloaks. Collecting in gangs as soon as dusk fell, they robbed their betters in the open Forum and in the narrow alleys, snatching from passersby their mantles, belts, gold brooches, and whatever they had in their hands. Some they killed after robbing them, so they could not inform anyone of the assault.

These outrages brought the enmity of everybody on them, especially that of the Blue partisans who had not taken active part in the discord. When even the latter were molested, they began to wear brass belts and brooches and cheaper cloaks than most of them were privileged to display, lest their elegance should lead to their deaths; and even before the sun went down they went home to hide. But the evil progressed; and as no punishment came to the criminals from those in charge of the public peace, their boldness increased more and more. For when crime finds itself licensed, there are no limits to its abuses; since even when it is punished, it is never quite suppressed, most men being by nature easily turned to error. Such, then, was the conduct of the Blues.

Some of the opposite party joined this faction so as to get even with the people of their original side who had ill-treated them; others fled in secret to other lands, but many were captured before they could get away, and perished either at the hands of their foes or by sentence of the State. And many other young men offered themselves to this society who had never before taken any interest in the quarrel, but were now induced by the power and possibility of insolence they could thus acquire. For there is no villainy to which men give a name that was not committed during this time, and remained unpunished.

Now at first they killed only their opponents. But as matters progressed, they also murdered men who had done nothing against them. And there were many who bribed them with money, pointing out personal enemies, whom the Blues straightway dispatched, declaring these victims were Greens, when as a matter of fact they were utter strangers. And all this went on not any longer at dark and by stealth, but in every hour of the day, everywhere in the city: before the eyes of the most notable men of the government, if they happened to be bystanders. For they did not need to conceal their crimes, having no fear of punishment, but considered it rather to the advantage of their reputation, as proving their strength and manhood, to kill with one stroke of the dagger any unarmed man who happened to be passing by.

No one could hope to live very long under this state of affairs, for everybody suspected he would be the next to be killed. No place was safe, no time of day offered any pledge of security, since these murders went on in the holiest of sanctuaries even during divine services. No confidence was left in one's friends or relatives, for many died by conspiracy of members of their own households. Nor was there any investigation after these deeds, but the blow would fall unexpectedly, and none avenged the victim. No longer was there left any force in law or contract, because of this disorder, but everything was settled by violence. The State might as well have been a tyranny: not one, however, that had been established, but one that was being overturned daily and ever recommencing.

The magistrates seemed to have been driven from their senses, and their wits enslaved by the fear of one man. The judges, when deciding cases that came up before them, cast their votes not according to what they thought right or lawful, but according as either of the disputants was an enemy or friend of the faction in power. For a judge who disregarded its instruction was sentencing himself to death. And many creditors were forced to receipt the bills they had sent to their debtors without being paid what was due them; and many thus against their will had to free their slaves.

And they say that certain ladies were forced by their own slaves to do what they did not want to do; and the sons of notable men, getting mixed up with these young bandits, compelled their fathers, among other acts against their will, to hand over their properties to them. Many boys were constrained, with their fathers' knowledge, to serve the unnatural desires of the Blues; and happily married women met the same misfortune.

It is told that a woman of no undue beauty was ferrying with her husband to the suburb opposite the mainland; when some men of this party met them on the water, and jumping into her boat, dragged her abusively from her husband and made her enter their vessel. She had whispered to her spouse to trust her and have no fear of any reproach, for she would not allow herself to be dishonored. Then, as he looked at her in great grief, she threw her body into the Bosphorus and forthwith vanished from the world of men. Such were the deeds this party dared to commit at that time in Constantinople.

Yet all of this disturbed people less than Justinian's offenses against the State. For those who suffer the most grievously from evildoers are relieved of the greater part of their anguish by the expectation they will sometime be avenged by law and authority. Men who are confident of the future can bear more easily and less painfully their present troubles; but when they are outraged even by the government what befalls them is naturally all the more grievous, and by the failing of all hope of redress they are turned to utter despair. And Justinian's crime was that he was not only unwilling to protect the injured, but saw no reason why he should not be the open head of the guilty faction; he gave great sums of money to these young men, and surrounded himself with them: and some he even went so far as to appoint to high office and other posts of honor.

## VIII. CHARACTER AND APPEARANCE OF JUSTINIAN

Now this went on not only in Constantinople, but in every city: for like any other disease, the evil, starting there, spread throughout the entire Roman Empire. But the Emperor was undisturbed by the trouble, even when it went on continually under his own eyes at the hippodrome. For he was very complacent and resembled most the silly ass, which follows, only shaking its ears, when one drags it by the bridle. As such Justinian acted, and threw everything into confusion.

As soon as he took over the rule from his uncle, his first measure was to spend the public money without restraint, now that he had control of it. He gave much of it to the Huns who, from time to time, entered the state; and in consequence the Roman provinces were subject to constant incursions, for these barbarians, having once tasted Roman wealth, never forgot the road that led to it. And he threw much money into the sea in the form of moles, as if to master the eternal roaring of the breakers. For he jealously hurled stone breakwaters far out from the mainland against the onset of the sea, as if by the power of wealth he could outmatch the might of ocean.

He gathered to himself the private estates of Roman citizens from all over the Empire: some by accusing their possessors of crimes of which they were innocent, others by juggling their owners' words into the semblance of a gift to him of their property. And many, caught in the act of murder and other crimes, turned their possessions over to him and thus escaped the penalty for their sins.

Others, fraudulently disputing title to lands happening to adjoin their own, when they saw they had no chance of getting the best of the argument, with the law against them, gave him their equity in the claim so as to be released from court. Thus, by a gesture that cost him nothing, they gained his favor and were able illegally to get the better of their opponents.

I think this is as good a time as any to describe the personal appearance of the man. Now in physique he was neither tall nor short, but of average height; not thin, but moderately plump; his face was round, and not bad looking, for he had good color, even when he fasted for two days. To make a long description short, he much resembled Domitian, Vespasian's son. He was the one whom the Romans so hated that even tearing him into pieces did not satisfy their wrath against him, but a decree was passed by the Senate that the name of this Emperor should never be written, and that no statue of him should be preserved. And so this name was erased in all the inscriptions at Rome and wherever else it had been written, except only where it occurs in the list of emperors; and nowhere may be seen any statue of him in all the Roman Empire, save one in brass, which was made for the following reason.

Domitian's wife was of free birth and otherwise noble; and neither had she herself ever done wrong to anybody, nor had she assented in her husband's acts. Wherefore she was dearly loved; and the Senate sent for her, when Domitian died, and commanded her to ask whatever boon she wished. But she asked only this: to set up in his memory one brass image, wherever she might desire. To this the Senate agreed. Now the lady, wishing to leave a memorial to future time of the savagery of those who had butchered her husband, conceived this plan: collecting the pieces of Domitian's body, she joined them accurately together and sewed the body up again into its original semblance. Taking this to the statue makers, she ordered them to produce the miserable form in brass. So the artisans forthwith made the image, and the wife took it, and set it up in the street which leads to the Capitol, on the right hand side as one goes there from the Forum: a monument to Domitian and a revelation of the manner of his death until this day.

Justinian's entire person, his manner of expression and all of his features might be clearly pointed out in this statue.

Now such was Justinian in appearance; but his character was something I could not fully describe. For he was at once villainous and amenable; as people say colloquially, a moron. He was never truthful with anyone, but always guileful in what he said and did, yet easily hoodwinked by any who wanted to deceive him. His nature was an unnatural mixture of folly and wickedness. What in olden times a peripatetic philosopher said was also true of him, that opposite qualities combine in a man as in the mixing of colors. I will try to portray him, however, insofar as I can fathom his complexity.

This Emperor, then, was deceitful, devious, false, hypocritical, two-faced, cruel, skilled in dissembling his thought, never moved to tears by either joy or pain, though he could summon them artfully at will when the occasion demanded, a liar always, not only offhand, but in writing, and when he swore sacred oaths to his subjects in their very hearing. Then he would immediately break his agreements and pledges, like the vilest of slaves, whom indeed only the fear of torture drives to confess their perjury. A faithless friend, he was a treacherous enemy, insane for murder and plunder, quarrelsome and revolutionary, easily led to anything evil, but never willing to listen to good counsel, quick to plan mischief and carry it out, but finding even the hearing of anything good distasteful to his ears.

How could anyone put Justinian's ways into words? These and many even worse vices were disclosed in him as in no other mortal: nature seemed to have taken the wickedness of all other men combined and planted it in this man's soul. And besides this, he was too prone to listen to accusations; and too quick to punish. For he decided such cases without full examination, naming the punishment when he had heard only the accuser's side of the matter. Without hesitation he wrote decrees for the plundering of countries, sacking of cities, and slavery of whole nations, for no cause whatever. So that if one wished to take all the calamities which had befallen the Romans before this time and weigh them against his crimes, I think it would be found that more men had been murdered by this single man than in all previous history.

He had no scruples about appropriating other people's property, and did not even think any excuse necessary, legal or illegal, for confiscating what did not belong to him. And when it was his, he was more than ready to squander it in insane display, or give it as an unnecessary bribe to the barbarians. In short, he neither held on to any money himself nor let anyone else keep any: as if his reason were not avarice, but jealousy of those who had riches. Driving all wealth from the country of the Romans in this manner, he became the cause of universal poverty.

Now this was the character of Justinian, so far as I can portray it.

## IX. HOW THEODORA, MOST DEPRAVED OF ALL COURTESANS, WON HIS LOVE

He took a wife: and in what manner she was born and bred, and, wedded to this man, tore up the Roman Empire by the very roots, I shall now relate.

Acacius was the keeper of wild beasts used in the amphitheater in Constantinople; he belonged to the Green faction and was nicknamed the Bearkeeper. This man, during the rule of Anastasius, fell sick and died, leaving three daughters named Comito, Theodora and Anastasia: of whom the eldest was not yet seven years old. His widow took a second husband, who with her undertook to keep up Acacius's family and profession. But Asterius, the dancing master of the Greens, on being bribed by another, removed this office from them and assigned it to the man who gave him the money. For the dancing masters had the power of distributing such positions as they wished.

When this woman saw the populace assembled in the amphitheater, she placed laurel wreaths on her daughters' heads and in their hands, and sent them out to sit on the ground in the attitude of suppliants. The Greens eyed this mute appeal with indifference; but the Blues were moved to bestow on the children an equal office, since their own animal-keeper had just died.

When these children reached the age of girlhood, their mother put them on the local stage, for they were fair to look upon; she sent them forth, however, not all at the same time, but as each one seemed to her to have reached a suitable age. Comito, indeed, had already become one of the leading hetaerae of the day.

Theodora, the second sister, dressed in a little tunic with sleeves, like a slave girl, waited on Comito and used to follow her about carrying on her shoulders the bench on which her favored sister was wont to sit at public gatherings. Now Theodora was still too young to know the normal relation of man with maid, but consented to the unnatural violence of villainous slaves who, following their masters to the theater, employed their leisure in this infamous manner. And for some time in a brothel she suffered such misuse.

But as soon as she arrived at the age of youth, and was now ready for the world, her mother put her on the stage. Forthwith, she became a courtesan, and such as the ancient Greeks used to call a common one, at that: for she was not a flute or harp player, nor was she even trained to dance, but only gave her youth to any-one she met, in utter abandonment. Her general favors included, of course, the actors in the theater; and in their productions she took part in the low comedy scenes. For she was very funny and a good mimic, and immediately became popular in this art. There was no shame in the girl, and no one ever saw her dismayed: no role was too scandalous for her to accept without a blush.

She was the kind of comedienne who delights the audience by letting herself be cuffed and slapped on the cheeks, and makes them guffaw by raising her skirts to reveal to the spectators those feminine secrets here and there which custom veils from the eyes of the opposite sex. With pretended laziness she mocked her lovers, and coquettishly adopting ever new ways of embracing, was able to keep in a constant turmoil the hearts of the sophisticated. And she did not wait to be asked by anyone she met, but on the contrary, with inviting jests and a comic flaunting of her skirts herself tempted all men who passed by, especially those who were adolescent.

On the field of pleasure she was never defeated. Often she would go picnicking with ten young men or more, in the flower of their strength and virility, and dallied with them all, the whole night through. When they wearied of the sport, she would approach their servants, perhaps thirty in number, and fight a duel with each of these; and even thus found no allayment of her craving. Once, visiting the house of an illustrious gentleman, they say she mounted the projecting corner of her dining couch, pulled up the front of her dress, without a blush, and thus carelessly showed her wantonness. And though she flung wide three gates to the ambassadors of Cupid, she lamented that nature had not similarly unlocked the straits of her bosom, that she might there have contrived a further welcome to his emissaries.

Frequently, she conceived, but as she employed every artifice immediately, a miscarriage was straightway effected. Often, even in the theater, in the sight of all the people, she removed her costume and stood nude in their midst, except for a girdle about the groin: not that she was abashed at revealing that, too, to the audience, but because there was a law against appearing altogether naked on the stage, without at least this much of a fig-leaf. Covered thus with a ribbon, she would sink down to the stage floor and recline on her back. Slaves to whom the duty was entrusted would then scatter grains of barley from above into the calyx of this passion flower, whence geese, trained for the purpose, would next pick the grains one by one with their bills and eat. When she rose, it was not with a blush, but she seemed rather to glory in the performance. For she was not only impudent herself, but endeavored to make everybody else as audacious. Often when she was alone with other actors, she would undress in their midst and arch her back provocatively, advertising like a peacock both to those who had experience of her and to those who had not yet had that privilege her trained suppleness.

So perverse was her wantonness that she should have hid not only the customary part of her person, as other women do, but her face as well. Thus those who were intimate with her were straightway recognized from that very fact to be perverts, and any more respectable man who chanced upon her in the Forum avoided her and withdrew in haste, lest the hem of his mantle, touching such a creature, might be thought to share in her pollution. For to those who saw her, especially at dawn, she was a bird of ill omen. And toward her fellow-actresses she was as savage as a scorpion: for she was very malicious.

Later, she followed Hecebolus, a Tyrian who had been made governor of Pentapolis, serving him in the basest of ways; but finally she quarreled with him and was sent summarily away. Consequently, she found herself destitute of the means of life, which she proceeded to earn by prostitution, as she had done before this adventure. She came thus to Alexandria, and then traversing all the East, worked her way to Constantinople; in every city plying a trade (which it is safer, I fancy, in the sight of God not to name too clearly) as if the Devil were determined there be no land on earth that should not know the sins of Theodora.

Thus was this woman born and bred, and her name was a byword beyond that of other common wenches on the tongues of all men.

But when she came back to Constantinople, Justinian fell violently in love with her. At first he kept her only as a mistress, though he raised her to patrician rank. Through him Theodora was able immediately to acquire an unholy power and exceedingly great riches. For she seemed to him the sweetest thing in the world, and like all lovers, he desired to please his charmer with every possible favor and requite her with all his wealth. The extravagance added fuel to the flames of passion. With her now to help spend his money he plundered the people more than ever, not only in the capital, but throughout the Roman Empire. As both of them had for a long time been of the Blue party, they gave this faction almost complete control of the affairs of state. It was long afterward that the worst of this evil was checked in the following manner.

Justinian had been ill for several days, and during this illness was in such peril of his life that it was even said he had died; and the Blues, who had been committing such crimes as I have mentioned, went so far as to kill Hypatius, a gentleman of no mean importance, in broad daylight in the Church of St. Sophia. The cry of horror at this crime came to the Emperor's ears, and everyone about him seized the opportunity of pointing out the enormity of what was going on in Justinian's absence from public affairs; and they enumerated from the beginning how many crimes had been committed. The Emperor then ordered the Prefect of the city to punish these offenses. This man was one Theodotus, nicknamed the Pumpkin. He made a thorough investigation and was able to apprehend many of the guilty and sentence them to death, though many others were not found out, and escaped. They were destined to perish later, together with the Roman Empire.

Justinian, unexpectedly restored to health, straightway undertook to put Theodotus to death as a poisoner and a magician. But since he had no proof on which to condemn the man, he tortured friends of his until they were compelled to say the words that would wrongfully ruin him. When everyone else stood to one side and only in silence lamented the plot against Theodotus, one man, Proclus the Quaestor, dared to say openly that the man was innocent of the charge against him, and in no way merited death. Thanks to him, Theodotus was permitted by the Emperor to be exiled to Jerusalem. But learning there that men were being sent to do away with him, he hid himself in the church for the rest of his life until he died. And this was the fate of Theodotus.

But after this, the Blues became the most prudent of men. For they ventured no longer to continue their offenses, even though they might have transgressed more fearlessly than before. And the proof of this is, that when a few of them later showed such courage, no punishment at all befell them. For those who had the power to punish, always gave these gangsters time to escape, tacitly encouraging the rest to trample upon the laws.

## X. HOW JUSTINIAN CREATED A NEW LAW PERMITTING HIM TO MARRY A COURTESAN

Now as long as the former Empress was alive, Justinian was unable to find a way to make Theodora his wedded wife. In this one matter she opposed him as in nothing else: for the lady abhorred vice, being a rustic and of barbarian descent, as I have shown. She was never able to do any real good, because of her continued ignorance of the affairs of state. She dropped her original name, for fear people would think it ridiculous, and adopted the name of Euphemia when she came to the palace. But finally her death removed this obstacle to Justinian's desire.

Justin, doting and utterly senile, was now the laughing stock of his subjects; he was disregarded by everyone because of his inability to oversee state affairs; but Justinian they all served with considerable awe. His hand was in everything, and his passion for turmoil created universal consternation.

It was then that he undertook to complete his marriage with Theodora. But as it was impossible for a man of senatorial rank to make a courtesan his wife, this being forbidden by ancient law, he made the Emperor nullify this ordinance by creating a new one, permitting him to wed Theodora, and consequently making it possible for anyone else to marry a courtesan. Immediately after this he seized the power of the Emperor, veiling his usurpation with a transparent pretext: for he was proclaimed colleague of his uncle as Emperor of the Romans by the questionable legality of an election inspired by terror.

So Justinian and Theodora ascended the imperial throne three days before Easter, a time, indeed, when even making visits or greeting one's friends is forbidden. And not many days later Justin died of an illness, after a reign of nine years. Justinian was now sole monarch, together, of course, with Theodora.

Thus it was that Theodora, though born and brought up as I have related, rose to royal dignity over all obstacles. For no thought of shame came to Justinian in marrying her, though he might have taken his pick of the noblest born, most highly educated, most modest, carefully nurtured, virtuous and beautiful virgins of all the ladies in the whole Roman Empire: a maiden, as they say, with upstanding breasts. Instead, he preferred to make his own what had been common to all men, and, careless of all her revealed history, took in wedlock a woman who was not only guilty of every other contamination but boasted of her many abortions.

I need hardly mention any other proof of the character of this man: for all the perversity of his soul was completely displayed in this union; which alone was ample interpreter, witness, and historian of his shamelessness. For when a man once disregards the disgrace of his actions and is willing to brave the contempt of society, no path of lawlessness is thereafter taboo to him; but with unflinching countenance he advances, easily and without a scruple, to acts of the deepest infamy.

However, not a single member of even the Senate, seeing this disgrace befalling the State, dared to complain or forbid the event; but all of them bowed down before her as if she were a goddess. Nor was there a priest who showed any resentment, but all hastened to greet her as Highness. And the populace who had seen her before on the stage, directly raised its hands to proclaim itself her slave in fact and in name. Nor did any soldier grumble at being ordered to risk the perils of war for the benefit of Theodora: nor was there any man on earth who ventured to oppose her.

Confronted with this disgrace, they all yielded, I suppose, to necessity; for it was as if Fate were giving proof of its power to control mortal affairs as malignantly as it pleases: showing that its decrees need not always be according to reason or human propriety. Thus does Destiny sometimes raise mortals suddenly to lofty heights in defiance of reason, in challenge to all outcries of injustice; but admits no obstacle, urging on his favorites to the appointed goal without let or hindrance. But as this is the will of God, so let it befall and be written.

Now Theodora was fair of face and of a very graceful, though small, person; her complexion was moderately colorful, if somewhat pale; and her eyes were dazzling and vivacious. All eternity would not be long enough to allow one to tell her escapades while she was on the stage, but the few details I have mentioned above should be sufficient to demonstrate the woman's character to future generations.

What she and her husband did together must now be briefly described: for neither did anything without the consent of the other. For some time it was generally supposed they were totally different in mind and action; but later it was revealed that their apparent disagreement had been arranged so that their subjects might not unanimously revolt against them, but instead be divided in opinion.

Thus they split the Christians into two parties, each pretending to take the part of one side, thus confusing both, as I shall soon show; and then they ruined both political factions. Theodora feigned to support the Blues with all her power, encouraging them to take the offensive against the opposing party and perform the most outrageous deeds of violence; while Justinian, affecting to be vexed and secretly jealous of her, also pretended he could not openly oppose her orders. And thus they gave the impression often that they were acting in opposition. Then he would rule that the Blues must be punished for their crimes, and she would angrily complain that against her will she was defeated by her husband. However, the Blue partisans, as I have said, seemed cautious, for they did not violate their neighbors as much as they might have done.

And in legal disputes each of the two would pretend to favor one of the litigants, and compel the man with

the worse case to win: and so they robbed both disputants of most of the property at issue.

In the same way, the Emperor, taking many persons
into his intimacy, gave them offices by power of which
they could defraud the State to the limits of their ambi-
tion. And as soon as they had collected enough plunder, they would fall out of favor with Theodora, and
straightway be ruined. At first he would affect great
sympathy in their behalf, but soon he would somehow
lose his confidence in them, and an air of doubt would
darken his zeal in their behalf. Then Theodora would
use them shamefully, while he, unconscious as it were
of what was being done to them, confiscated their
properties and boldly enjoyed their wealth. By such
well-planned hypocrisies they confused the public and,
pretending to be at variance with each other, were able
to establish a firm and mutual tyranny.

## XI. HOW THE DEFENDER
## OF THE FAITH
## RUINED HIS SUBJECTS

As soon as Justinian came into power he turned everything upside down. Whatever had before been forbidden by law he now introduced into the government,
while he revoked all established customs: as if he had
been given the robes of an Emperor on the condition
he would turn everything topsy-turvy. Existing offices
he abolished, and invented new ones for the management of public affairs. He did the same thing to the
laws and to the regulations of the army; and his reason
was not any improvement of justice or any advantage,
but simply that everything might be new and named
after himself. And whatever was beyond his power to
abolish, he renamed after himself anyway.

Of the plundering of property or the murder of men,
no weariness ever overtook him. As soon as he had
looted all the houses of the wealthy, he looked around
for others; meanwhile throwing away the spoils of his
previous robberies in subsidies to barbarians or senseless
building extravagances. And when he had ruined perhaps myriads in this mad looting, he immediately sat
down to plan how he could do likewise to others in
even greater number.

As the Romans were now at peace with all the world
and he had no other means of satisfying his lust for
slaughter, he set the barbarians all to fighting each
other. And for no reason at all he sent for the Hun

chieftains, and with idiotic magnanimity gave them large sums of money, alleging he did this to secure their friendship. This, as I have said, he had also done in Justin's time. These Huns, as soon as they had got this money, sent it together with their soldiers to others of their chieftains, with the word to make inroads into the land of the Emperor: so that they might collect further tribute from him, to buy them off in a second peace. Thus the Huns enslaved the Roman Empire, and were paid by the Emperor to keep on doing it.

This encouraged still others of them to rob the poor Romans; and after their pillaging, they too were further rewarded by the gracious Emperor. In this way all the Huns, for when it was not one tribe of them it was another, continuously overran and laid waste the Empire. For the barbarians were led by many different chieftains, and the war, thanks to Justinian's senseless generosity, was thus endlessly protracted. Consequently no place, mountain or cave, or any other spot in Roman territory, during this time remained uninjured; and many regions were pillaged more than five times.

These misfortunes, and those that were caused by the Medes, Saracens, Slavs, Antes, and the rest of the barbarians, I described in my previous works. But, as I said in the preface to this narrative, the real cause of these calamities remained to be told here.

To Chosroes also he paid many centenaries in behalf of peace, and then with unreasonable arbitrariness caused the breaking of the truce by making every effort to secure the friendship of Alamandur and his Huns, who had been in alliance with the Persians: but this I freely discussed in my chapters on the subject.

Moreover, while he was encouraging civil strife and frontier warfare to confound the Romans, with only one thought in his mind, that the earth should run red with human blood and he might acquire more and more booty, he invented a new means of murdering his subjects. Now among the Christians in the entire Roman Empire, there are many with dissenting doctrines, which are called heresies by the established church: such as those of the Montanists and Sabbatians, and whatever others cause the minds of men to wander from the true path. All of these beliefs he ordered to be abolished, and their place taken by the orthodox dogma: threatening, among the punishments for disobedience, loss of the heretic's right to will property to his children or other relatives.

Now the churches of these so-called heretics, especially those belonging to the Arian dissenters, were almost incredibly wealthy. Neither all the Senate put together nor the greatest other unit of the Roman Empire, had anything in property comparable to that of these churches. For their gold and silver treasures, and stores of precious stones, were beyond telling or numbering: they owned mansions and whole villages, land all over the world, and everything else that is counted as wealth among men.

As none of the previous Emperors had molested these churches, many men, even those of the orthodox faith, got their livelihood by working on their estates. But the Emperor Justinian, in confiscating these properties, at the same time took away what for many people had been their only means of earning a living.

Agents were sent everywhere to force whomever they

chanced upon to renounce the faith of their fathers. This, which seemed impious to rustic people, caused them to rebel against those who gave them such an order. Thus many perished at the hands of the persecuting faction, and others did away with themselves, foolishly thinking this the holier course of two evils; but most of them by far quitted the land of their fathers, and fled the country. The Montanists, who dwelt in Phrygia, shut themselves up in their churches, set them on fire, and ascended to glory in the flames. And thenceforth the whole Roman Empire was a scene of massacre and flight.

A similar law was then passed against the Samaritans, which threw Palestine into an indescribable turmoil. Those, indeed, who lived in my own Caesarea and in the other cities, deciding it silly to suffer harsh treatment over a ridiculous trifle of dogma, took the name of Christians in exchange for the one they had borne before, by which precaution they were able to avoid the perils of the new law. The most reputable and better class of these citizens, once they had adopted this religion, decided to remain faithful to it; the majority, however, as if in spite for having not voluntarily, but by the compulsion of law, abandoned the belief of their fathers, soon slipped away into the Manichean sect and what is known as polytheism.

The country people, however, banded together and determined to take arms against the Emperor: choosing as their candidate for the throne a bandit named Julian, son of Sabarus. And for a time they held their own against the imperial troops; but finally, defeated in battle, were cut down, together with their leader.

Ten myriads of men are said to have perished in this engagement, and the most fertile country on earth thus became destitute of farmers. To the Christian owners of these lands, the affair brought great hardship: for while their profits from these properties were annihilated, they had to pay heavy annual taxes on them to the Emperor for the rest of their lives, and secured no remission of this burden.

Next he turned his attention to those called Gentiles, torturing their persons and plundering their lands. Of this group, those who decided to become nominal Christians saved themselves for the time being; but it was not long before these, too, were caught performing libations and sacrifices and other unholy rites. And how he treated the Christians shall be told hereafter.

After this he passed a law prohibiting pederasty: a law pointed not at offenses committed after this decree, but at those who could be convicted of having practised the vice in the past. The conduct of the prosecution was utterly illegal. Sentence was passed when there was no accuser: the word of one man or boy, and that perhaps a slave, compelled against his will to bear witness against his owner, was defined as sufficient evidence. Those who were convicted were castrated and then exhibited in a public parade. At the start, this persecution was directed only at those who were of the Green party, were reputed to be especially wealthy, or had otherwise aroused jealousy.

The Emperor's malice was also directed against the astrologer. Accordingly, magistrates appointed to punish thieves also abused the astrologers, for no other reason than that they belonged to this profession; whipping them on the back and parading them on camels throughout the city, though they were old men, and in every way respectable, with no reproach against them except that they studied the science of the stars while living in such a city.

Consequently there was a constant stream of emigration not only to the land of the barbarians but to places farthest remote from the Romans; and in every country and city one could see crowds of foreigners. For in order to escape persecution, each would lightly exchange his native land for another, as if his own country had been taken by an enemy.

## XII. PROVING THAT JUSTINIAN AND THEODORA WERE ACTUALLY FIENDS IN HUMAN FORM

Now the wealth of those in Constantinople and each other city who were considered second in prosperity only to members of the Senate, was brutally confiscated, in the ways I have described, by Justinian and Theodora. But how they were able to rob even the Senate of all its property I shall now reveal.

There was in Constantinople a man by the name of Zeno, grandson of that Anthamius who had formerly been Emperor of the West. This man they appointed, with malice aforethought, Governor of Egypt, and commanded his immediate departure. But he delayed his voyage long enough to load his ship with his most valuable effects; for he had a countless amount of silver and gold plate inlaid with pearls, emeralds and other such precious stones. Whereupon they bribed some of his most trusted servants to remove these valuables from the ship as fast as they could carry them, set fire to the interior of the vessel, and inform Zeno that his ship had burst into flames of spontaneous combustion, with the loss of all his property. Later, when Zeno died suddenly, they took possession of his estate immediately as his legal heirs; for they produced a will which, it is whispered, he did not really make.

In the same manner they made themselves heirs of Tatian, Demosthenes, and Hilara, who were foremost in the Roman Senate. And others' estates they obtained by counterfeited letters instead of wills. Thus they became heirs of Dionysius, who lived in Libanus, and of John the son of Basil, who was the most notable of the citizens of Edessa, and had been given as hostage, against his will, by Belisarius to the Persians: as I have recounted elsewhere. For Chosroes refused to let this John go, charging that the Romans had disregarded the terms of the truce, as a pledge of which John had been given him by Belisarius; and he said he would only give him up as a prisoner of war. So his father's mother, who was still living, got together a ransom not less than two thousand pounds of silver, and was ready to purchase her grandson's liberty. But when this money came to Dara, the Emperor heard of the bargain and forbade it: saying that Roman wealth must not be given to the barbarians. Not long after this, John fell ill and departed from this world, whereupon the Governor of the city forged a letter which, he said, John had written him as a friend not long before, to the effect that he wished his estate to go to the Emperor.

I could hardly catalogue all the other people whose estates these two chose to inherit. However, up to the time when the insurrection named Nika took place, they seized rich men's properties one at a time; but when that happened, as I have told elsewhere, they sequestrated at one swoop the estates of nearly all the members of the Senate. On everything movable and on the fairest of the lands they laid their hands and kept what they wanted; but whatever was unproductive of more than the bitter and heavy taxes, they gave back to the previous owners with a philanthropic gesture. Consequently these unfortunates, oppressed by the tax collectors and eaten up by the never-ceasing interest on their debts, found life a burden compared to which death were preferable.

Wherefore to me, and many others of us, these two seemed not to be human beings, but veritable demons, and what the poets call vampires: who laid their heads together to see how they could most easily and quickly destroy the race and deeds of men; and assuming human bodies, became man-demons, and so convulsed the world. And one could find evidence of this in many things, but especially in the superhuman power with which they worked their will.

For when one examines closely, there is a clear difference between what is human and what is supernatural. There have been many enough men, during the whole course of history, who by chance or by nature have inspired great fear, ruining cities or countries or whatever else fell into their power; but to destroy all men and bring calamity on the whole inhabited earth remained for these two to accomplish, whom Fate aided in their schemes of corrupting all mankind. For by earthquakes, pestilences, and floods of river waters at this time came further ruin, as I shall presently show. Thus not by human, but by some other kind of power they accomplished their dreadful designs.

And they say his mother said to some of her intimates once that not of Sabbatius her husband, nor of any man was Justinian a son. For when she was about to conceive, there visited a demon, invisible but giving evidence of his presence perceptibly where man consorts with woman, after which he vanished utterly as in a dream.

And some of those who have been with Justinian at the palace late at night, men who were pure of spirit, have thought they saw a strange demoniac form taking his place. One man said that the Emperor suddenly rose from his throne and walked about, and indeed he was never wont to remain sitting for long, and immediately Justinian's head vanished, while the rest of his body seemed to ebb and flow; whereat the beholder stood aghast and fearful, wondering if his eyes were deceiving him. But presently he perceived the vanished head filling out and joining the body again as strangely as it had left it.

Another said he stood beside the Emperor as he sat, and of a sudden the face changed into a shapeless mass of flesh, with neither eyebrows nor eyes in their proper places, nor any other distinguishing feature; and after a time the natural appearance of his countenance returned. I write these instances not as one who saw them myself, but heard them from men who were positive they had seen these strange occurrences at the time.

They also say that a certain monk, very dear to God, at the instance of those who dwelt with him in the desert went to Constantinople to beg for mercy to his neighbors who had been outraged beyond endurance. And when he arrived there, he forthwith secured an audience with the Emperor; but just as he was about to enter his apartment, he stopped short as his feet were on the threshold, and suddenly stepped backward. Whereupon the eunuch escorting him, and others who were present, importuned him to go ahead. But he answered not a word; and like a man who has had a stroke staggered back to his lodging. And when some followed to ask why he acted thus, they say he distinctly declared he saw the King of the Devils sitting on the throne in the palace, and he did not care to meet or ask any favor of him.

Indeed, how was this man likely to be anything but an evil spirit, who never knew honest satiety of drink or food or sleep, but only tasting at random from the meals that were set before him, roamed the palace at unseemly hours of the night, and was possessed by the quenchless lust of a demon?

Furthermore some of Theodora's lovers, while she was on the stage, say that at night a demon would sometimes descend upon them and drive them from the room, so that it might spend the night with her. And there was a certain dancer named Macedonia, who belonged to the Blue party in Antioch, who came to possess much influence. For she used to write letters to Justinian while Justin was still Emperor, and so made away with whatever notable men in the East she had a grudge against, and had their property confiscated.

This Macedonia, they say, greeted Theodora at the time of her arrival from Egypt and Libya; and when she saw her badly worried and cast down at the ill treatment she had received from Hecebolus and at the loss of her money during this adventure, she tried to encourage Theodora by reminding her of the laws of chance, by which she was likely again to be the leader of a chorus of coins. Then, they say, Theodora used to relate how on that very night a dream came to her, bidding her take no thought of money, for when she should come to Constantinople, she should share the couch of the King of the Devils, and that she should contrive to become his wedded wife and thereafter be the mistress of all the money in the world. And that this is what happened is the opinion of most people.

## XIII. DECEPTIVE
AFFABILITY AND
PIETY OF A
TYRANT

Justinian, while otherwise of such character as I have shown, did make himself easy of access and affable to his visitors; nobody of all those who sought audience with him was ever denied: even those who confronted him improperly or noisily never made him angry. On the other hand, he never blushed at the murders he committed. Thus he never revealed a sign of wrath or irritation at any offender, but with a gentle countenance and unruffled brow gave the order to destroy myriads of innocent men, to sack cities, to confiscate any amount of properties.

One would think from this manner that the man had the mind of a lamb. If, however, anyone tried to propitiate him and in suppliance beg him to forgive his victims, he would grin like a wild beast, and woe betide those who saw his teeth thus bared!

The priests he permitted fearlessly to outrage their neighbors, and even took sympathetic pleasure in their robberies, fancying he was thus sharing their divine piety. When he judged such cases, he thought he was doing the holy thing when he gave the decision to the priest and let him go free with his ill-gotten booty: justice, in his mind, meant the priests' getting the better of their opponents. When he himself thus illegally got possession of estates of people alive or dead, he would straightway make them over to one of the churches, gilding his violence with the color of piety—and so that his victims could not possibly get their property back. Furthermore he committed an inconceivable number of murders for the same cause: for in his zeal to gather all men into one Christian doctrine, he recklessly killed all who dissented, and this too he did in the name of piety. For he did not call it homicide, when those who perished happened to be of a belief that was different from his own.

So quenchless was his thirst for human blood; and with his wife, intent on this end, he neglected no possible excuse for slaughter. For these two were almost twins in their desires, though they pretended to differ: they were both scoundrels, however they affected to oppose each other, and thus destroyed their subjects. The man was lighter in character than a cloud of dust, and could be led to do anything any man wished him to do, so long as the matter did not require philanthropy or generosity. Flattery he swallowed whole, and his courtiers had no difficulty in persuading him that he was destined to rise as high as the sun and walk upon the clouds.

Once, indeed, Tribonian, who was sitting beside him, said his greatest fear was that Justinian some day by reason of his piety would be carried off to heaven and vanish in a chariot of fire. Such praise, if not irony, as this he treasured fondly in his mind.

Yet if he ever remarked on any man's virtue, he would soon revile him as a villain; and whenever he abused any of his subjects, he would next as inconsistently commend him, with no reason for the change.

For what he thought was always the opposite of what he said and wished to seem to think.

How he was affected by friendship or enmity I have indicated by the evidence of his actions. For as a foe he was relentless and unswerving, and to his friends he was inconstant. Thus he ruined recklessly most of those who were loyal to him, but never became a friend to any whom he hated. Even those who seemed to be his nearest and dearest associates he betrayed, and after no long time, to please his wife or anybody else, though he was well aware that it was only because of their devotion to him that they perished. For he was openly faithless in everything, except indeed to inhumanity and avarice. From these ideals no man could divert him. Whatever his wife could not otherwise induce him to do, by suggesting the great profits to be hoped for in the matter she intended, she led him quite willingly to undertake. For if there were any gain in it, however infamous, he had no scruple against making a law and then repudiating it. Nor were his decisions made according to the laws himself had written: but whichever way was to his greater advantage, and promised the more elaborate bribe. Stealing, little by little, the property of his subjects, he saw no reason for feeling any shame; when, indeed, he did not somehow grab it all at once, either by bringing some unexpected accusation or by presenting a forged will.

There remained, while he ruled the Romans, no sure faith in God, no hope in religion, no defense in law, no security in business, no trust in a contract. When his officials were given any affair to handle for him, if they killed many of their victims and robbed the rest, they were looked upon by the Emperor with high favor, and given honorable mention for carrying out so perfectly his instructions. But if they showed any mercy and then returned to him, he frowned and was thenceforth their enemy.

Despising their qualms as old-fashioned, he called them no more to his service. Consequently many were eager to show him how wicked they were, even when they were really nothing of the sort. He made frequent promises, guaranteed with a sworn oath or by a written confirmation; and then purposely forgot them directly, thinking this summary negligence added to his importance. And Justinian acted thus not only to his subjects, but to many of the enemy, as I have already said.

He was untiring; and hardly slept at all, generally speaking; he had no appetite for food or drink, but picking up a morsel with the tips of his fingers, tasted it and left the table, as if eating were a duty imposed upon him by nature and of no more interest than a courier takes in delivering a letter. Indeed, he would often go without food for two days and nights, especially when the time before the festival called Easter enjoins such fasting. Then, as I have said, he often went without food for two days, living only on a little water and a few wild herbs, sleeping perhaps a single hour, and then spending the rest of the time walking up and down.

If, mark you, he had spent these periods in good works, matters might have been considerably alleviated. Instead, he devoted the full strength of his nature to the ruin of the Romans, and succeeded in razing the state to its foundation. For his constant wakefulness, his privations and his labors were undergone for no other reason than to contrive each day ever more exaggerated calamities for his people. For he was, as I said, unusually keen at inventing and quick at accomplishing unholy acts, so that even the good in him transpired to be answerable for the downfall of his subjects.

## XIV. JUSTICE FOR SALE

Everything was done the wrong way, and of the old customs none remained; a few instances will illustrate, and the rest must be silence, that this book may have an end. In the first place, Justinian, having no natural aptitude toward the imperial dignity, neither assumed the royal manner nor thought it necessary to his prestige. In his accent, in his dress, and in his ideas he was a barbarian. When he wished to issue a decree, he did not give it out through the Quaestor's office, as is usual, but most frequently preferred to announce it himself, in spite of his barbarous accent; or sometimes he had a whole group of his intimates publish it together, so that those who were wronged by the edict did not know which one to complain against.

The secretaries who had performed this duty for centuries were no longer trusted with writing the Emperor's secret dispatches: he wrote them himself and practically everything else, too; so that in the few cases where he neglected to give instructions to city magistrates, they did not know where to go for advice concerning their duties. For he let no one in the Roman Empire decide anything independently, but taking everything upon himself with senseless arrogance, gave the verdict in cases before they came to trial, accepting the story of one of the litigants without listening to the other, and then pronounced the argument concluded; swayed not by any law or justice, but openly yielding to base greed. In accepting bribes the Emperor felt no shame, since hunger for wealth had devoured his decency.

Often the decrees of the Senate and those of the Emperor nominally conflicted. The Senate, however, sat only for pictorial effect, with no power to vote or do anything. It was assembled as a matter of form, to comply with the ancient law, and none of its members was permitted to utter a single word. The Emperor and his Consort took upon themselves the decisions of all matters in dispute, and their will of course prevailed. And if anybody thought his victory in such a case was insecure because it was illegal, he had only to give the Emperor more money, and a new law would immediately be passed revoking the former one. And if anybody else preferred the law that had been repealed, the ruler was quite willing to reestablish it in the same manner.

Under this reign of violence nothing was stable, but the balance of justice revolved in a circle, inclining to whichever side was able to weight it with the heavier amount of gold. Publicly in the Forum, and under the management of palace officials, the selling of court decisions and legislative actions was carried on.

The officers called Referendars were no longer satisfied to perform their duties of presenting to the Emperor the request of petitioners, and referring to the magistrates what he had decided in the petitioner's case; but gathering worthless testimony from all quarters, with false reports and misleading statements, deceived Justinian, who was naturally inclined to listen to that sort of thing; and then they would go back to the litigants, without telling them what had been said during their interview with the Emperor, to extort as much money as they desired. And no one dared oppose them.

The soldiers of the pretorian guard, attending the judges of the imperial court in the palace, also used their power to influence decisions. Everybody, one might say, stepped from his rank and found he was now at liberty to walk roads where before there had been no path; all bars were down, even the names of former restrictions were lost. The government was like a Queen surrounded by romping children. But I must pass over further illustrations, as I said at the beginning of this chapter.

I must, however, mention the man who first taught the Emperor to sell his decisions. This was Leo, a native of Cilicia, and devilish eager to enrich himself. This Leo was the prince of flatterers, and apt at insinuating himself into the good will of the ignorant. Gaining the confidence of the Emperor, he turned the tyrant's folly toward the ruin of the people. This man was the first to show Justinian how to exchange justice for money.

As soon as the latter thus learned how to be a thief, he never stopped; but advancing on this road, the evil grew so great that if anyone wished to win an unjust case against an honest man, he went first to Leo, and agreeing that a share of the disputed property would be given to be divided between this man and the monarch, left the palace with his wrongful case already won. And Leo soon built up a great fortune in this way, became the lord of much land, and was most responsible for bringing the Roman state to its knees.

There was no security in contracts, no law, no oath, no written pledge, no penalty, no nothing: unless money had first been given to Leo and the Emperor. And even buying Leo's support gave no certainty, for Justinian was quite willing to take money from both sides: he felt no guilt at robbing either party, and then, when both trusted him, he would betray one and keep his promise to the other, at random. He saw nothing disgraceful in such double dealing, if only it brought him gain. That is the sort of person Justinian was.

## XV. HOW ALL ROMAN CITIZENS BECAME SLAVES

Theodora too unceasingly hardened her heart in the practice of inhumanity. What she did, was never to please or obey anyone else; what she willed, she performed of her own accord and with all her might: and no one dared to intercede for any who fell in her way. For neither length of time, fulness of punishment, artifice of prayer, nor threat of death, whose vengeance sent by Heaven is feared by all mankind, could persuade her to abate her wrath. Indeed, no one ever saw Theodora reconciled to any one who had offended her, either while he lived or after he had departed this earth. Instead, the son of the dead would inherit the enmity of the Empress, together with the rest of his father's estate: and he in turn bequeathed it to the third generation. For her spirit was over ready to be kindled to the destruction of men, while cure for her fever there was none.

To her body she gave greater care than was necessary, if less than she thought desirable. For early she entered the bath and late she left it; and having bathed, went to breakfast. After breakfast she rested. At dinner and supper she partook of every kind of food and drink; and many hours she devoted to sleep, by day till nightfall, by night till the rising sun. Though she wasted her hours thus intemperately, what time of the day remained she deemed ample for managing the Roman Empire.

And if the Emperor intrusted any business to anyone without consulting her, the result of the affair for that officer would be his early and violent removal from favor and a most shameful death.

It was easy for Justinian to look after everything, not only because of his calmness of temper, but because he hardly ever slept, as I have said, and because he was not chary with his audiences. For great opportunity was given to people, however obscure and unknown, not only to be admitted to the tyrant's presence, but to converse with him, and in private.

But to the Queen's presence even the highest officials could not enter without great delay and trouble; like slaves they had to wait all day in a small and stuffy antechamber, for to absent himself was a risk no official dared to take. So they stood there on their tiptoes, each straining to keep his face above his neighbor's, so that eunuchs, as they came out from the audience room, would see them. Some would be called, perhaps, after several days; and when they did enter to her presence in great fear, they were quickly dismissed as soon as they had made obeisance and kissed her feet. For to speak or make any request, unless she commanded, was not permitted.

Not civility, but servility was now the rule, and Theodora was the slave driver. So far had Roman society been corrupted, between the false geniality of the tyrant and the harsh implacability of his consort. For his smile was not to be trusted, and against her frown nothing could be done. There was this superficial difference between them in attitude and manner; but in avarice, bloodthirstiness, and dissimulation they utterly agreed. They were both liars of the first water.

And if any one who had fallen out of favor with Theodora was accused of some minor and insignificant error, she immediately fabricated further unwarranted charges against the man, and built the matter up into a really serious accusation. Any number of indictments were brought, and a court appointed to plunder the victim, with judges selected by her, to compete with themselves to see which one could please her most in fitting his decision to the Empress's inhumanity. And so the property of the victim would be straightway confiscated, and after he was cruelly whipped, even if he perhaps belonged to an ancient and noble family, she would callously have him sentenced to exile or to death.

But if any of her favorites happened to be caught in the act of murder or any other serious crime, she ridiculed and belittled the efforts of their accusers, and compelled them, however unwillingly, to quash the charge. Indeed, whenever she felt the inclination, she turned the most serious matters of state into a jest, as if she were again on the stage of the theater.

Once an elderly patrician, who had been for a long time in high office (whose name I well know, but shall carefully refrain from mentioning, so as not to bring eternal ridicule upon him), being unable to collect from one of her attendants a considerable sum of money owed him, went to her with the intention of asking his due and imploring her just aid. But Theodora was warned, and told her eunuchs, as soon as the patrician should be admitted to her presence, to surround him in a body and listen to her words; telling them what to say after she had spoken. And when the patrician was admitted to her private quarters, he kissed her feet in the customary manner and, weeping, addressed her:

"Highness, it is hard for a patrician to ask for money. For what in other men brings sympathy and pity, in one of my rank is considered disgraceful. Any other man suffering hardships from poverty may plead this before his creditors, and receive immediate relief from his difficulty; but a patrician, not knowing whence he can find the wherewithal to pay his creditors, would be ashamed in the first place to admit it. And if he did say this, he could never persuade them that one of such rank could know penury. And even if he did persuade them, he would be making himself suffer the most shameful and intolerable disgrace imaginable.

"Yet, Highness, such is my plight. I have creditors to whom I owe money, while others owe money to me. And those whom I owe, who are pressing me for payment, I cannot, for the sake of my reputation, attempt to cheat of their due; while my debtors, for they are not patricians, deny me with unmanly excuses. I charge you, therefore; I beseech and beg of you, to aid me in what is right, and release me from my present trouble."

So he said, and the Queen answered musically:

"Patrician Mr. Such-and-such—"

whereupon the chorus of eunuchs sang:

"Your hernia seems to bother you much!"

And when the man entreated her again, making a second speech similar to his first one, she answered as before, and the chorus sang the same refrain: till, giving it up, the poor wretch bowed and went home.

Most of the year the Empress resided in the suburbs on the seashore, especially in the place called Heraeum, and the numerous crowd of her attendants was subjected to great inconvenience. For it was hard to get necessary supplies, and they were exposed to the perils of the sea: especially to the frequent sudden storms and the attack of sharks. Nevertheless they counted the most bitter misfortunes as nothing, so long as they could share the licenses of her court.

## XVI. WHAT HAPPENED TO THOSE WHO FELL OUT OF FAVOR WITH THEODORA

How Theodora treated those who offended her will now be shown, though again I can give only a few instances, or obviously there would be no end to the demonstration.

When Amasalontha decided to save her life by surrendering her queendom over the Goths and retiring to Constantinople (as I have related elsewhere), Theodora, reflecting that the lady was well-born and a Queen, more than easy to look at and a marvel at planning intrigues, became suspicious of her charms and audacity: and fearing her husband's fickleness, she became not a little jealous, and determined to ensnare the lady to her doom.

So she forthwith persuaded Justinian to send Peter, alone, to Italy as ambassador to Theodatus. When he set out the Emperor gave him the instructions I described in the chapter on that event: where, however, I could not tell the whole truth of the matter, for fear of the Empress. But she gave him this single secret command: to remove the lady from this world with all dispatch; bribing the fellow with the hope of much money if he performed his order. And when he arrived in Italy (for man is not by nature too hesitant at committing murder, if he has been bribed by the promise of high office or considerable money), by what argument I know not, he persuaded Theodatus to make away with Amasalontha. Consequently raised to the rank of Master of Offices, he achieved immense power and universal hatred. And so ends the story of Amasalontha.

Then there was a secretary to Justinian named Priscus: an utter villain and Paphlagonian, of a character likely to please his master, to whom he was more than devoted, and from whom he expected similar consideration. And accordingly he very soon became the owner of great and ill-gotten wealth. Finding him insolent and always trying to oppose her, Theodora denounced him to the Emperor. At first she was unsuccessful; but before long she took the matter in her own hands: embarked the man on a ship, sailing to a determined port, had his head shaved, and compelled him against his will to become a priest. And Justinian, pretending he knew nothing of the matter, never asked where on earth Priscus was, nor ever after mentioned him: remaining silent as if he had utterly forgotten him. However, he did not forget to seize what property Priscus had been forced to abandon.

Again, Theodora was overtaken with suspicion of one of her servants named Areobindus, a barbarian by birth, but a handsome young man, whom she had made her steward. Instead of accusing him directly, she decided to have him cruelly whipped in her presence (though they say she was madly in love with the fellow) without explaining her reason for the punishment. What became of the man after that we do not know, nor has any one ever seen him since. For if the Queen wanted to keep any of her actions concealed, it remained secret and unmentioned; and neither was any who knew of the matter allowed to tell it to his closest friend, nor could any who tried to learn what had happened ever find out, no matter how much of a busybody he was.

No other tyrant since mankind began ever inspired such fear, since not a word could be spoken against her without her hearing of it: her multitude of spies brought her the news of whatever was said and done in public or in private. And when she decided the time had come to take vengeance on any offender, she did as follows. Summoning the man, if he happened to be notable, she would privately hand him over to one of her confidential attendants, and order that he be escorted to the farthest boundary of the Roman realm. And her agent, in the dead of night, covering the victim's face with a hood and binding him, would put him on board a ship and accompany him to the place selected by Theodora. There he would secretly leave the unfortunate in charge of another qualified for this work: charging him to keep the prisoner under guard and tell no one of the matter until the Empress should take pity on the wretch or, as time went on, he should languish under his bondage and succumb to death.

Then there was Basanius, one of the Green faction, a prominent young man, who incurred her anger by making some uncomplimentary remark. Basanius, warned of her displeasure, fled to the Church of Michael the Archangel. She immediately sent the Prefect after him, charging Basanius however not with slander, but pederasty. And the Prefect, dragging the man from the church, had him flogged intolerably while all the populace, when they saw a Roman citizen of good standing so shamefully mistreated, straightway sympathized with him, and cried so loud to let him go that Heaven must have heard their reproaches. Whereupon the Empress punished him further, and had him castrated so that he bled to death, and his estate was confiscated; though his case had never been tried. Thus, when this female was enraged, no church offered sanctuary, no law gave protection, no intercession of the people brought mercy to her victim; nor could anything else in the world stop her.

Thus she took a hatred of a certain Diogenes, because he belonged to the Greens: a man urbane and beloved by all, including the Emperor himself. None the less she wrathfully denounced him as homosexual. Bribing two of his servants, she presented them as accusers and witnesses against their master. However, as he was tried publicly and not in secret, as was her usual practise in such cases, the judges chosen were many and of distinguished character, because of Diogenes's high rank; and after cross-examination of the evidence of the servants, they decided it was insufficient to prove the case, especially as the latter were only children.

So the Empress locked up Theodorus, one of Diogenes's friends, in one of her private dungeons; and there first with flattery, then with flogging, tried to overwhelm him. When he still resisted, she ordered a cord of oxhide to be wound around his head and then turned and tightened. But though they twisted the cord till his eyes started from their sockets and Theodora thought he would lose them completely, still he refused to confess what he had not done. Accordingly the judges, for lack of proof, acquitted him, while all the city took holiday to celebrate his release. And that was that.

## XVII. HOW SHE SAVED FIVE HUNDRED HARLOTS FROM A LIFE OF SIN

I have told earlier in this narrative what she did to Belisarius, Photius and Buzes.

There were two members of the Blue faction, Cilicians by birth, who with a mob of others offered violence to Callinicus, Governor of the second Cilicia; and when his groom, who was standing near his master, tried to protect him, they slew the fellow before the eyes of the Governor and all the people. The Governor, convicting the two of this and many previous murders, sentenced them to death. Theodora heard of this, and to show her preference for the Blues, crucified Callinicus, without troubling to remove him from his office, on the spot where the murderers had been buried.

The Emperor affected to lament and mourn the death of his Governor, and sat around grumbling and making threats against those responsible for the deed. But he did nothing, except to seize the estate of the dead man.

Theodora also devoted considerable attention to the punishment of women caught in carnal sin. She picked up more than five hundred harlots in the Forum, who earned a miserable living by selling themselves there for three obols, and sent them to the opposite mainland, where they were locked up in the monastery called Repentance to force them to reform their way of life. Some of them, however, threw themselves from the parapets at night and thus freed themselves from an undesired salvation.

There were in Constantinople two girls: sisters, of a very illustrious family—not only had their father and grandfather been Consuls, but even before that their ancestors had been Senators. These girls had both married early, but became widows when their husbands died; and immediately Theodora, accusing them of living too merrily, chose new husbands for them, two common and disgusting fellows, and commanded the marriage to take place. Fearing this repulsive fate, the sisters fled to the Church of St. Sophia, and running to the holy water, clung tightly to the font. Yet such privations and ill treatment did the Empress inflict upon them there, that to escape from their sufferings they finally agreed to accept the proposed nuptials. For no place was sacred or inviolable to Theodora. Thus involuntarily these ladies were mated to beggarly and negligible men, far beneath their rank, although they had many well-born suitors. Their mother, who was also a widow, attended the ceremony without daring to protest or even weep at their misfortune.

Later Theodora saw her mistake and tried to console them, to the public detriment, for she made their new husbands Dukes. Even this brought no comfort to the young women, for endless and intolerable woes were inflicted on practically all their subjects by these men; as I have told elsewhere. Theodora, however, cared nothing for the interest of office or government, or anything else, if only she accomplished her will.

She had accidentally become pregnant by one of her lovers, when she was still on the stage; and perceiving her ill luck too late, tried all the usual measures to cause a miscarriage, but despite every artifice was unable to prevail against nature at this advanced stage of development. Finding that nothing else could be done, she abandoned the attempt and was compelled to give birth to the child. The father of the baby, seeing that Theodora was at her wit's end and vexed because motherhood interfered with her usual recreations, and suspecting with good reason that she would do away with the child, took the infant from her, naming him John, and sailed with the baby to Arabia. Later, when he was on the verge of death and John was a lad of fourteen, the father told him the whole story about his mother.

So the boy, after he had performed the last rites for his departed father, shortly after came to Constantinople and announced his presence to the Empress's chamberlains. And they, not conceiving the possibility of her acting so inhumanly, reported to the mother that her son John had come. Fearing the story would get to the ears of her husband, Theodora bade her son be brought face to face with her. As soon as he entered, she handed him over to one of her servants who was ordinarily entrusted with such commissions. And in what manner the poor lad was removed from the world, I cannot say, for no one has ever seen him since, not even after the Queen died. The ladies of the court at this time were nearly all of abandoned morals. They ran no risk in being faithless to their husbands, as the sin brought no penalty: even if caught in the act, they were unpunished, for all they had to do was to go to the Empress, claim the charge was not proven, and start a countersuit against their husbands. The latter, defeated without a trial, had to pay a fine of twice the dower, and were usually whipped and sent to prison; and the next time they saw their adulterous wives again, the ladies would be daintily entertaining their lovers more openly than ever. Indeed, many of the latter gained promotion and pay for their amorous services. After one such experience, most men who suffered these outrages from their wives preferred thereafter to be complaisant instead of being whipped, and gave them every liberty rather than seem to be spying on their affairs.

Theodora's idea was to control everything in the state to suit herself. Civil and ecclesiastical offices were all in her hands, and there was only one thing she was always careful to inquire about and guard as the standard of her appointments: that no honest gentleman should be given high rank, for fear he would have scruples against obeying her commands.

She arranged all marriages as if that were her divine right, and voluntary betrothals before a ceremony were unknown. A wife would suddenly be found for a man, chosen not because she pleased him, which is customary even among the barbarians, but because Theodora willed it. And the same was true of brides, who were forced to take men they did not desire. Frequently she even made the bride jump out of her marriage bed, and for no reason at all sent the bridegroom away before he had reached the chorus of his nuptial song; and her only angry words would be that the girl displeased her. Among the many to whom she did this were Leontius, the Referendar, and Saturninus, the son of Hermogenes the Master of Offices.

Now this Saturninus was betrothed to a maiden cousin, freeborn and a good girl, whom her father Cyril had promised him in marriage just after the death of Hermogenes. When their bridal chamber was in readiness, Theodora arrested the groom, who was conducted to another nuptial couch, where, weeping and groaning terribly, he was compelled to wed Chrysomallo's daughter. Chrysomallo herself had formerly been a dancer and a hetaera; at this time she lived in the palace, with another woman of the same name and one called Indaro, having given up Cupid and the stage to be of service to the Queen.

Saturninus, lying down finally to pleasant dreams with his new bride, discovered she was already un-maidened; and later told one of his friends that his new-found mate came to him not imperforate. When this comment got to Theodora, she ordered her servants, charging him with impious disregard of the solemnity of his matrimonial oath, to hoist him up like a schoolboy who had been saucy to his teacher: and after whipping him on his backsides, told him not to be such a fool thereafter.

What she did to John the Cappadocian I have told elsewhere; and need add only that her treatment of him was due to her anger, not at his transgressions against the state (and a proof of this is that those who later did even more terrible things to their subjects met no such similar fate from her), but because he had not only dared oppose her in other things, but had denounced her before the Emperor: with the result that she was all but estranged from her husband. I am explaining this now, for it is in this book, as I said in the foreword, that I necessarily tell the real truths and motives of events.

When she confined him in Egypt, after he had suffered such humiliations as I have previously described, she was not even then satisfied with the man's punishment, but never ceased hunting for false witnesses against him. Four years later, she was able to find two members of the Green party who had taken part in the insurrection at Cyzicus, and who were said to have shared in the assault upon the bishop. These two she overwhelmed with flattery and threats, and one of them, inspired by her promises, accused John of the murder; while the other utterly refused to be an accomplice in this libel, even when he was so injured by the torture that he seemed about to die on the spot. Consequently for all her efforts she was unable to cause John's death on this pretext. But the two young men had their right hands cut off: one, because he was unwilling to bear false witness; the other, that her conspiracy might not be utterly obvious. Thus she was able to do things in full public sight, and still nobody knew exactly what she had done.

## XVIII. HOW JUSTINIAN KILLED A TRILLION PEOPLE

That Justinian was not a man, but a demon, as I have said, in human form, one might prove by considering the enormity of the evils he brought upon mankind. For in the monstrousness of his actions the power of a fiend is manifest. Certainly an accurate reckoning of all those whom he destroyed would be impossible, I think, for anyone but God to make. Sooner could one number, I fancy, the sands of the sea than the men this Emperor murdered. Examining the countries that he made desolate of inhabitants, I would say he slew a trillion people. For Libya, vast as it is, he so devastated that you would have to go a long way to find a single man, and he would be remarkable. Yet eighty thousand Vandals capable of bearing arms had dwelt there, and as for their wives and children and servants, who could guess their number? Yet still more numerous than these were the Mauretanians, who with their wives and children were all exterminated. And again, many Roman soldiers and those who followed them to Constantinople, the earth now covers; so that if one should venture to say that five million men perished in Libya alone, he would not, I imagine, be telling the half of it.

The reason for this was that after the Vandals were defeated, Justinian planned, not how he might best strengthen his hold on the country, nor how by safeguarding the interests of those who were loyal to him he might have the goodwill of his subjects: but instead he foolishly recalled Belisarius at once, on the charge that the latter intended to make himself King (an idea of which Belisarius was utterly incapable), and so that he might manage affairs there himself and be able to plunder the whole of Libya. Sending commissioners to value the province, he imposed grievous taxes where before there had been none. Whatever lands were most valuable, he seized, and prohibited the Arians from observing their religious ceremonies. Negligent toward sending necessary supplies to the soldiers, he was overstrict with them in other ways; wherefore mutinies arose resulting in the deaths of many. For he was never able to abide by established customs, but naturally threw everything into confusion and disturbance.

Italy, which is not less than thrice as large as Libya, was everywhere desolated of men, even worse than the other country; and from this the count of those who perished there may be imagined. The reason for what happened in Italy I have already made plain. All of his crimes in Libya were repeated here; sending his auditors to Italy, he soon upset and ruined everything.

The rule of the Goths, before this war, had extended from the land of the Gauls to the boundaries of Dacia, where the city of Sirmium is. The Germans held Cisalpine Gaul and most of the land of the Venetians, when the Roman army arrived in Italy. Sirmium and the neighboring country was in the hands of the Gepidae. All of these he utterly depopulated. For those who did not die in battle perished of disease and famine, which as usual followed in the train of war. Illyria and all of Thrace, that is, from the Ionian Gulf to the suburbs of Constantinople, including Greece and the Chersonese, were overrun by the Huns, Slavs and Antes, almost every year, from the time when Justinian took over the Roman Empire; and intolerable things they did to the inhabitants. For in each of these incursions, I should say, more than two hundred thousand Romans were slain or enslaved, so that all this country became a desert like that of Scythia.

Such were the results of the wars in Libya and in Europe. Meanwhile the Saracens were continuously making inroads on the Romans of the East, from the land of Egypt to the boundaries of Persia; and so completely did their work, that in all this country few were left, and it will never be possible, I fear, to find out how many thus perished. Also the Persians under

Chosroes three times invaded the rest of this Roman territory, sacked the cities, and either killing or carrying away the men they captured in the cities and country, emptied the land of inhabitants every time they invaded it. From the time when they invaded Colchis, ruin has befallen themselves and the Lazi and the Romans.

For neither the Persians nor the Saracens, the Huns or the Slavs or the rest of the barbarians, were able to withdraw from Roman territory undamaged. In their inroads, and still more in their sieges of cities and in battles, where they prevailed over opposing forces, they shared in disastrous losses quite as much. Not only the Romans, but nearly all the barbarians thus felt Justinian's bloodthirstiness. For while Chosroes himself was bad enough, as I have duly shown elsewhere, Justinian was the one who each time gave him an occasion for the war. For he took no heed to fit his policies to an appropriate time, but did everything at the wrong moment: in time of peace or truce he ever craftily contrived to find pretext for war with his neighbors; while in time of war, he unreasonably lost interest, and hesitated too long in preparing for the campaign, grudging the necessary expenses; and instead of putting his mind on the war, gave his attention to stargazing and research as to the nature of God. Yet he would not abandon hostilities, since he was so bloodthirsty and tyrannical, even when thus unable to conquer the enemy because of his negligence in meeting the situation.

So while he was Emperor, the whole earth ran red with the blood of nearly all the Romans and the barbarians. Such were the results of the wars throughout the whole Empire during this time. But the civil strife in Constantinople and in every other city, if the dead were reckoned, would total no smaller number of slain than those who perished in the wars, I believe. Since justice and impartial punishment were seldom directed against offenders, and each of the two factions tried to win the favor of the Emperor over the other, neither party kept the peace. Each, according to his smile or his frown, was now terrified, now encouraged. Sometimes they attacked each other in full strength, sometimes in smaller groups, or even lay in ambush against the first single man of the opposite party who came along. For thirty-two years, without ever ceasing, they performed outrages against each other, many of them being punished with death by the municipal Prefect.

However, punishment for these offenses was mostly directed against the Greens.

Furthermore the persecution of the Samaritans and the so-called heretics filled the Roman realm with blood. Let this present recapitulation suffice to recall what I have described more fully a little while since. Such were the things done to all mankind by the demon in flesh for which Justinian, as Emperor, was responsible. But what evils he wrought against men by some hidden power and diabolic force I shall now relate.

During his rule over the Romans, many disasters of various kinds occurred: which some said were due to the presence and artifices of the Devil, and others considered were effected by the Divinity, Who, disgusted with the Roman Empire, had turned away from it and given the country up to the Old One. The Scirtus River flooded Edessa, creating countless sufferings among the inhabitants, as I have elsewhere written. The Nile, rising as usual, but not subsiding in the customary season, brought terrible calamities to the people there, as I have also previously recounted. The Cydnus inundated Tarsus, covering almost the whole city for many days, and did not subside until it had done irreparable damage.

Earthquakes destroyed Antioch, the leading city of the East; Seleucia, which is situated nearby; and Anazarbus, most renowned city in Cilicia. Who could number those that perished in these metropoles? Yet one must add also those who lived in Ibora; in Amasea, the chief city of Pontus; in Polybotus in Phrygia, called Polymede by the Pisidians; in Lychnidus in Epirus; and in Corinth: all thickly inhabited cities from of old. All of these were destroyed by earthquakes during this time, with a loss of almost all their inhabitants. And then came the plague, which I have previously mentioned, killing half at least of those who had survived the earthquakes. To so many men came their doom, when Justinian first came to direct the Roman state and later possessed the throne of autocracy.

## XIX. HOW HE SEIZED ALL THE WEALTH OF THE ROMANS AND THREW IT AWAY

How he seized all wealth I will next discuss: recalling first a vision which, at the beginning of Justinian's rule, was revealed to one of illustrious rank in a dream.

In this dream, he said, he seemed to be standing on the shore of the sea somewhere in Constantinople, across the water from Chalcedon, and saw Justinian there in midchannel. And first Justinian drank up all the water of the sea, so that he presently appeared to be standing on the mainland, there being no longer any waves to break against it; then other water, heavy with filth and rubbish, roaring out of the subterranean sewers, proceeded to cover the land. And this, too, he drank, a second time drying up the bed of the channel. This is what the vision in the dream disclosed.

Now Justinian, when his uncle Justin came to the throne, found the state well provided with public funds. For Anastasius, who had been the most provident and economical of all monarchs, fearing (which indeed happened) that the inheritor of his Empire should find himself in need of money, would perhaps plunder his subjects, filled all the treasuries to their brim with gold before he completed his span of life. All of this Justinian immediately exhausted, between his senseless building program on the coast and his lavish presents to the barbarians; though one might have thought that it would take the most extragavant of Emperors a hundred years to disburse such wealth. For the treasurers and those in charge of the other imperial properties had been able, during Anastasius's rule of more than twenty-seven years over the Romans, easily to accumulate 3,200 gold centenaries; and of all these nothing at all was left, for it had been squandered by this man while Justin still lived; as I have already related.

What he illegally confiscated and wasted during his lifetime, no tale, no reckoning, no count could ever make manifest. For like an everflowing river swallowing more each day he pillaged his subjects, to disgorge it straightway on the barbarians.

Having thus carried away the public wealth, he turned his eye upon his private subjects. Most of them he immediately robbed of their estates, snatching them arbitrarily by force, bringing false charges against whoever in Constantinople and each other city were reputed to be rich.

Some he accused of polytheism, others of heresy against the orthodox Christian faith; some of pederasty, others of love affairs with nuns, or other unlawful intercourse; some of starting sedition, or of favoring the Greens, or treason against himself, or anything else; or he made himself the arbitrary heir of the dead and even of the living, when he could. Such were the subtleties of his actions. And how he profited from the insurrection against himself which is called Nika, making himself heir to the Senators, I have already shown; and how, some time before the sedition broke out, he privately robbed each man of his estate.

To all the barbarians, on every occasion, he gave great sums: to those of the East and those of the West, to the North and to the South, as far as Britain, and over all the inhabited earth; so that nations whose very names we had never heard of, we now learned to know, seeing their ambassadors for the first time. For when they learned of this man's folly, they came to him and Constantinople in floods from the whole world. And he with no hesitation, but overjoyed at this, and thinking it good luck to drain the Romans of their prosperity and fling it to barbarian men or to the waves of the sea, daily sent each one home with his arms full of presents.

Thus all the barbarians became masters of all the wealth of the Romans, either being presented with it by the Emperor, or by ravaging the Roman Empire, selling their prisoners for ransom, and bartering for truces. And the prophecy of the dream I mentioned above, came to pass in this visible reality.

## XX. DEBASING OF THE QUAESTORSHIP

He also had contrived other ways of plundering his subjects (which I will now describe as well as I can) by which he robbed them, not all at once, but little by little of their entire fortunes. First he appointed a new municipal magistrate, with the power to license shopkeepers to sell their wares at whatever prices they desired: for which privilege they paid an annual tax. Accordingly, people buying their provisions in these shops had to pay three times what the stuff was worth, and complainants had no redress, though great harm was thus done; for the magistrates saw to it that the imperial tax was fattened accordingly, which was to their advantage. Thus the government officials shared in this disgraceful business, while the shopkeepers, empowered to act illegally, cheated unbearably those who had to buy from them, not only by raising their prices many times over, as I have said, but by defrauding customers in other unheard-of ways.

Again he licensed many monopolies, as they are called; selling the freedom of his subjects to those who were willing to undertake this reprehensible traffic, after he had exacted his price for the privilege. To those who made this arrangement with him, he gave the power to manage the business however they pleased; and he sold this privilege openly, even to all the other magistrates. And since the Emperor always got his little share of the plundering, these officials and their subordinates in charge of the work, did their robbing with small anxiety.

As if the formerly appointed magistrates were not enough for this purpose, he created two new ones; though the municipal Prefect had formerly been able to look after all criminal charges. His real reason for the change was, of course, so that he could have additional informers, and thus misuse the innocent with more celerity. Of the two new officials, one, nominally appointed to punish thieves, was called Praetor of the People; the other was charged with the punishment of cases of pederasty, illegal intercourse with women, blasphemy, and heresy; and his official name was Quaestor.

Now the Praetor, whenever he found anything very valuable among the stolen goods that came to his notice, was supposed to give it to the Emperor and say that no owner had appeared to claim it. In this way the Emperor continually got possession of priceless goods. And the Quaestor, when he condemned persons coming before him, confiscated as much as he pleased of their properties, and the Emperor shared with him each time in the lawlessly gained riches of other people. For the subordinates of these magistrates neither produced accusers nor offered witnesses when these cases came to trial, but during all this time the accused were put to death, and their properties seized without due trial and examination.

Later, this murdering devil ordered these officials and the municipal Prefect to deal with all criminal charges on equal terms: telling them to vie with each other to see which of them could destroy the most people in the shortest time. And one of them asked him at once, they say, "If somebody is sometime denounced before all three of us, which of us shall have jurisdiction over the case?" Whereupon he replied, "Whichever of you acts faster than the rest."

Thus shamelessly he debased the Quaestor's office, which former emperors almost without exception had held in high regard, taking care that the men they appointed to it were experienced and wise, law-abiding, and uncorruptible by bribes; since otherwise it would be a calamity to the state, if men holding this high office were ignorant or avaricious.

But the first man that this Emperor appointed to the office was Tribonian, whose actions I have fully related elsewhere. And when Tribonian departed from this world, Justinian seized a portion of his estate, though a son and many other children were left destitute when the fellow ended the final day of his life. Junilus, a Libyan, was next appointed to this office: a man who had never even heard the law, for he was not a rhetorician; he knew the Latin letters, but as far as Greek went, he had never even gone to school, and was unable to speak the language. Frequently when he tried to say a Greek word, he was laughed at by his servants. And he was so damned greedy for base gain, that he thought nothing of publicly selling the Emperor's decrees. For one gold coin he would hold out his palm to anybody without hesitation. And for not less than seven years' time the State shared the ridicule earned by this petty grafter.

When Junilus completed the measure of his life, Constantine was appointed Quaestor: a man not un-

acquainted with law, but exceeding young, and without actual experience in court; and the most thievish
bully among men. Of this person Justinian was very
fond, and became his bosom friend, since through him
the Emperor saw he could steal and run the office as
he wished. Consequently, Constantine had great wealth
in a short time, and assumed an air of prodigious pomp,
with his nose in the clouds despising all men; and even
those who wanted to offer him large bribes had to
entrust them to those who were in his special confidence, to offer him together with their requests; for
it was never possible to meet or talk with him, except
when he was running to the Emperor or had just left
him, and even then he trotted by in a great hurry, lest
his time be wasted by somebody who had no money to
give him. This is what the Emperor did to the quaestor-
ship.

## XXI. THE SKY TAX, AND HOW BORDER ARMIES WERE FORBIDDEN TO PUNISH INVADING BARBARIANS

The Prefect in charge of the praetors each year handed over to the Emperor more than thirty centenaries in addition to the public taxes; this tribute was called the sky tax, to show, I suppose, that it was not a regular duty or assessment, but as it were fell into his hands by chance out of the sky: it should have been called the villainy tax, for in its name the magistrates robbed their subjects worse than ever, on the ground they had to hand it over to the autocrat, while they themselves acquired a king's fortune in no time. For this Justinian left them unpunished, awaiting the time when they should have gained immense riches; as soon as this happened, he brought some charge against them for which there was no defense, and confiscated their entire property all at once, as he had done to John of Cappadocia.

Everyone appointed to office during this period of course became immensely wealthy at once, with two exceptions: Phocas, whom I have mentioned elsewhere as an utterly honest man, who remained uncorrupted by gain during his office; and Bassus, who was appointed later. Neither of these gentlemen held their office for a year, but were removed after a few months

as useless and unsuited to the times. But if I went into
all the details, this book would never end: suffice it to
say that all the rest of the magistrates in Constantinople
were equally guilty.

Also everywhere else in the Roman Empire Justinian
did the same. Picking out the worst scoundrels he could
find, he sold them the offices they were to corrupt, for
large sums of money. Indeed, an honest man or one
with any sense at all, would never think of throwing
away his own money on the chance of getting it back
by robbing the innocent. When Justinian had collected
this money from such bargainers, he gave them complete power over their subjects, by which, pillaging the
country and the inhabitants, they were to become rich.
And since they had borrowed money at heavy interest
to pay the Emperor for their magistracies, as soon as
they arrived in the cities of their jurisdiction, they
treated their subjects with every kind of evil, caring for
nothing but how they might fulfill their agreements
with their creditors and themselves thereafter be listed
among the super-wealthy. They saw no peril and felt
no shame in this conduct; rather, they anticipated that
the more they wrongfully killed and plundered, the
higher would be their reputation; for the name of mur-
derer and robber would prove the energy of their service. However, as soon as he heard these officials had
become adequately wealthy, Justinian snared them
with a fitting pretext, and straightway seized their
fortunes in one swoop.

He passed a law that candidates for offices must
swear they would keep themselves clean of all graft
and never give or receive any bribe as officials; and all

the curses that were named by the ancients he invoked on any who should violate this agreement. But the law was not over a year old before he himself, disregarding its words and maledictions, shamelessly put these offices up for sale; and not secretly, but in the public Forum. And the buyers of the offices, breaking their oaths also, plundered more than ever.

Later he contrived another unheard-of scheme. The offices which he believed to be the most powerful in Constantinople and the other large cities, he decided not to sell any longer as he had been doing, but put them in the hands of picked men on a fixed salary, who were commanded to turn over all revenues to himself. And these men, after receiving their pay, worked fearlessly and carried off everything on earth, going around in the name of their office to rob the subjects.

The Emperor was always very careful to choose for his agents men who were truly of all people the worst scoundrels; and he had no trouble finding those who were bad enough. When, indeed he appointed the first rascals to office, and their power brought to light their corruption, we were astonished that nature had produced such evil in human form. But when the successors to these offices later went far beyond the first occupants in villainy, men were at a loss to see how their predecessors could have been thought to be wicked, since in comparison to the new officials the former had been noble gentlemen in their actions. And the third set, and those who followed them, out-Heroded the second lot in every kind of depravity; and by their ingenuity in inventing new methods of bringing false charges, gave all their predecessors the name of being virtuous and honest. As the evil progressed, it was eventually demonstrated that the wickedness of man has no natural limit, but when it feeds on the experience of the past, and is given the opportunity to mistreat its victims, it is encouraged to such a degree that only those who are oppressed by it can measure it. And thus were the Romans treated by their magistrates.

After armies of the hostile Huns had several times enslaved and plundered inhabitants of the Roman Empire, the Thracian and Illyrian generals planned to attack them on their retreat, but gave up the idea when they were shown letters from the Emperor Justinian forbidding them to attack the barbarians on the ground that alliance with them was necessary to the Romans against the Goths, forsooth, or some other foe.

And after this, these barbarians ravaged the country as if they were the foe, and enslaved the Romans there; and, laden with booty and captives, these friends and allies of the Romans returned to their homes. Often some of the farmers of these regions, induced by longing for their children and wives who had been carried off to slavery, formed into bands and attacked the Huns, killing many, and capturing their horses laden with spoils; but the consequence of their success was unfortunate. For agents were sent from Constantinople to beat and torture them and seize their property, until they had given up all the horses they had taken from the barbarians.

## XXII. FURTHER
## CORRUPTION IN
## HIGH PLACES

Now when the Emperor and Theodora dismissed John of Cappadocia, they wished to appoint a successor to his office, and agreed to choose a still baser rogue; so they looked everywhere for such an instrument of tyranny, examining all manner of men that they might be able to ruin their subjects the faster. For the time being, they appointed Theodotus to the office: a man who was by no means good, but still not bad enough to satisfy them; and meanwhile they continued their general search till finally, almost to their surprise, they discovered a banker named Peter, a Syrian by birth, surnamed Barsyames; who, after years of sitting at the copper money-changer's table had made himself rich by thievish malpractices, being gifted at stealing obols, which he could filch under the eyes of customers by the quickness of his fingers. He was not only smart at this sleight-of-hand thievery, but if he were ever detected, would swear it was a mistake, covering up the sins of his hands with the impudence of his tongue.

Enlisting in the pretorian guard, he behaved so outrageously that Theodora was delighted with him, and decided he could most easily serve her in the worst of her nefarious schemes. So Theodotus, who had succeeded the Cappadocian, was straightway removed from office and Peter appointed in his place; and he did everything to their taste. Cheating all the soldiers of their due pay, without the slightest shame or fear, he also offered offices for sale to a greater extent than ever to those who did not hesitate to engage in this impious traffic for dishonored positions; and he openly licensed those who bought these offices to use as they wished the lives and substance of their subjects. For he claimed himself, and granted to whoever paid the price of a province, the right to destroy and ravage without restriction.

This sale of human lives proceeded from the first officer of the State; and by him the contract for the ruin of cities was made. Through the principal law-courts and in the public Forum went the licensed bandit who was given the name of Collector—collector of the money paid for high offices which was in turn extorted from the despairing people. And of all the imperial agents, many of whom were men of repute, Peter selected for his own service those who were villains.

In this he was not unique; for those who held the same office before and after him were equally dishonest. So were the Master of Offices, the Palatine Treasurers of the public and the Emperor's private moneys, and those in charge of his personal estates; and, in short, all who held public offices in Constantinople and the other cities. For from the time when this tyrant first managed the affairs of state, in each department the ministers without any justification claimed the moneys pertaining to that department for themselves, whenever he did not take them himself; and the subordinates of these officials, suffering the extremes of penury during all this time, were compelled to serve in the manner of slaves.

Most of the great stores of grain that had been kept in Constantinople had rotted; but he forced each of the cities of the East to buy what was not fit for human consumption; and he made them pay not what was the usual price for the best grain, but a still higher rate; so that the purchasers who had thrown away large sums of money, buying at such extravagant prices, had then to throw the rotten grain into the sea or down the sewers. Then the grain that was still sound and wholesome, of which there was great abundance, he decided to sell to the cities that were in danger of famine. In this way he made twice the money which the public collectors had formerly taken by the sale of this grain.

The next year, however, the harvests were not so ample, and the grain transports arrived at Constantinople with less than the necessary supply. Peter, worried over the situation, determined to buy a large quantity of grain in Bithynia, Phrygia, and Thrace. So the inhabitants of these regions were forced to the heavy task of bringing their harvests down to the seacoast and to transport it at considerable peril to Constantinople, where they received a miserably small price. So great indeed were their losses, that they would have been glad to give their grain outright to the State and pay a fine for that privilege. This is the grievous burden which was called "co-operative buying."

But when even thus the supplies of grain in Constantinople were insufficient for its needs, many de-

nounced this system before the Emperor. And at the
same time nearly all the soldiers, because they had not
been given their due pay, assembled mutinously
throughout the city and created a great uproar. The
Emperor turned now against Peter and decided to remove him from office, because of the above-mentioned
complaints, and since he heard he had hidden a devil-
ishly large amount of plunder of which he had robbed
the State. Which was indeed the case.

But Theodora would not let her husband do this, for
she was marvelously delighted with Barsyames, I suppose because of his wickedness and his remarkable
cruelty to his subjects. For she herself was utterly
savage and bursting with inhumanity, and thought
those who served her should be as nearly as possible
of a character with herself. They say, too, that she had
been involuntarily charmed by magic to become Peter's
friend; for this Barsyames was a devotee of sorcerers
and demons, and was admittedly a member of the
Manichaeans. Although the Empress had heard all this,
she did not withdraw her favor from the man, but
decided to prefer and favor him all the more on this
account. For she herself from childhood had consorted
with magicians and sorcerers, as her pursuits inclined
her toward them, and all her life she believed in the
black art and had great confidence in it.

They even say that it was not so much by flattery that
she made Justinian eat from her hand as by demoniac
power. For this was not a kindly, just, or good man,
to prevail over such machinations, but plainly over-
mastered by his passion for murder and money; easily

yielding to those who deceived and flattered him, and in the midst of his fondest plans he could be diverted with facility, like a bit of dust caught up by the wind. None of his kindred or his friends had any sure confidence in him, and his plans were continually subject to change. Thus, he was an easy mark to sorcery, as I have said, and with no difficulty fell into the power of Theodora. And it was for this reason that the Empress regarded Peter, practised in such arts, with great affection.

So it was all the Emperor could do to remove him from office; and at Theodora's insistence, soon afterward he made him chief of the treasurers, removing John from this position which he had given him only a few months before. This man John was a native of Palestine, exceedingly good and gentle, ignorant of the possibility of increasing his private fortune, and had never wronged a single man. All the people loved him; and therefore he could not please Justinian and his wife, who, as soon as they saw among their agents an unexpected decent gentleman, became faint with horror, and determined to get rid of him at the first possible opportunity.

So it was that Peter succeeded John as chief of the treasurers, and once more became the cause of great calamities. Embezzling most of the moneys which had been set apart since the time of a long-past Emperor to be distributed each year to the many poor, he made himself thus unjustly rich at the expense of the people, and handed a share of it to the Emperor. Those who were thus deprived of their dole sat around in great grief. Furthermore, he did not coin the customary amount of gold, but issued a less amount, a thing that had never happened before. And this is how the Emperor dealt with the magistracies.

## XXIII. HOW LAND-OWNERS WERE RUINED

I will now tell how he ruined the landowners everywhere; although it were a sufficient indication of their sufferings to refer to what I have just written about the officials who were sent to all the cities, for these men plundered the landowners and did what other violence has been told.

Now it had formerly been the long-established custom that each Roman ruler should, not only once during his reign but often remit to his subjects whatever public debts were in arrears, so that those who were in financial difficulty and had no means of paying their delinquencies would not be too far pressed; and so that the tax collectors would not have the excuse of persecuting, as subject to the tax, those who really owed nothing. But Justinian, during thirty-two years' time, made no such concession to his subjects, and consequently those who were unable to pay had to flee their country and never return. Others, more prosperous, grew weary of trying to answer the continual accusations of the informers that the tax they had always paid was less than required by the present rate on their estates. For these unfortunates feared not so much the imposition of a new tax as that they should be burdened by the unjust weight of additional back taxes for so many years. Many, indeed, preferred to abandon their property to the informers or to the confiscation of the state.

Besides, the Medes and the Saracens had ravaged most of Asia, and the Huns and Slavs all of Europe; captured cities had either been razed to their foundations, or made to pay terrible tribute; men had been carried off into slavery together with all their property, and every district had been deserted by its inhabitants because of the daily raids: yet no tax was remitted, except in the case of cities that had been captured by the enemy, and then only for one year. Yet if, as the Emperor Anastasius had done, he had decided to exempt the captured cities from taxation for seven years, even so, I believe, he would not have done as much as he should.

For Cabades retired after doing hardly any damage to the buildings, but Chosroes burned to the foundations everything he took, and left greater ruin in his track. Yet to these remaining sufferers, for whom he made this ridiculous remission of taxes, and to all the others, who had many times been invaded by the army of the Medes, and been continually plundered by the Huns and barbarous Saracens in the East, and to those Romans who had met an equal fate daily from the barbarians in Europe, this Emperor straightway became a more bitter foe than all the barbarians put together. For as soon as the enemy had retreated, the landowners immediately were overwhelmed by new requisitions, imposts and levies.

What these were I will now explain. Those who owned land were compelled to feed the Roman army, according to a special assessment determined by the actual emergency but arbitrarily fixed by law. And if sufficient provisions for the soldiers and horses were not to be found on their estates, these unfortunates had to go out and buy them at an excessive price, wherever they could, even if they had to transport them from a distant country to the place where the army was quartered, and then distribute them to the army officials not at a legal price, but at the whim of the commanders. This requisition, called co-operative buying, took the heart out of the landowners. For it made their annual taxes easily ten times what they had been, as they had not only to feed the army, but often to transport grain from Constantinople. Barsyames was not the only one who dared this outrage, for the Cappadocian before him had done the same, and Barsyames's successors after him. And this is what co-operative buying meant.

The "impost" was an unexpected ruin which suddenly attacked the landowners, pulling up their hope of livelihood by the roots. In the case of estates that had run down and been deserted, whose owners and farmer tenants had either perished or left the country, on account of their misfortunes, and disappeared, a ruthless tax was still laid on those who had already lost all. This was called the impost, levied frequently during this time.

The nature of the third levy was briefly as follows: Many losses, especially at this time, were suffered by the cities, whose causes and extents I refrain from describing now, or the tale would be endless. These losses the landowners had to repair, by special assessment on each individual; and their troubles did not even stop there. The pestilence, which had attacked the inhabited world, did not spare the Roman Empire. Most of its farmers had perished of it, so that their lands were deserted; nevertheless Justinian did not exempt the owners of these properties. Their annual taxes were not remitted, and they had to pay not only their own, but their deceased neighbors' share. And in addition to all of this, these land-poor wretches had to quarter the soldiers in their best rooms, while they themselves during this time existed in the meanest and poorest part of their dwellings.

Such were the constant afflictions of mankind under the rule of Justinian and Theodora; for there was no release from war or any other of these calamities in all their time.

While I am on the subject of quartering, I should not fail to mention that the householders in Constantinople had to quarter seventy thousand barbarians, so that they got no pleasure from their own houses, and were greatly inconvenienced in many ways.

## XXIV. UNJUST
## TREATMENT OF
## THE SOLDIERS

I must not pass over his treatment of the soldiers, over whom he appointed paymasters with instructions to hold out as much of their money as they found possible, on the understanding that one twelfth of what they thus collected was theirs. Their method each year was as follows. It was the regulation that different ranks in the army receive different pay: the young and newly enlisted received less, those who had seen hard service and had advanced half way up the list received more, and the veterans who should soon retire from service had a still higher rating, so that they could live on their savings as private citizens, and when their span of life was complete, might be able to leave some consolation to their families. In this way, the soldiers step by step arose in rank as their older comrades died or retired, and each man's pay fitted his degree of seniority.

But the paymasters forbade the erasing from the lists of the names of soldiers who died, even when many perished together, as frequently happened in the constant wars. Nor did they fill the vacancies in the lists, even after considerable time.

The result of this was that the number of soldiers grew continually less, and those who survived their dead comrades were deprived of their proper advancement in rank and pay; while the paymasters handed over to Justinian the money that should have gone to these soldiers all this time.

Furthermore, they fined the soldiers for other personal and unjust reasons, as a reward for the perils they underwent in the battlefield: on the charge that they were Greeks, as if none of that nation could be brave; or that they were not commissioned by the Emperor to serve, even when they showed his signature to that effect, which the paymasters did not hesitate to question; or that they had been absent from duty for a few days.

Later, some of the palace guards were sent throughout the whole Roman Empire to investigate how many on the military lists were unfit for service; and some were relieved of their uniform for being old and useless, so that for the rest of their lives they had to beg their meals of the charitable in the public Forum, exhibiting their tears and lamentations to passersby; and the rest, lest they might suffer a similar fate, handed over their savings as a bribe, with the result that all the soldiers lost heart for their profession, were reduced to poverty, and had no further enthusiasm for campaigning.

This was ruinous to the Romans and their authority in Italy; and the paymaster Alexander, sent thither, had the audacity to reproach the soldiers for their poor morale; while he exacted further money from the Italians, on the pretext of punishing them for their negotiations with Theodoric and the Goths. The common soldiers, indeed, were not the only ones to be reduced to poverty and helplessness by these commissioners; for all the staff officers, under the generals, who had formerly been in high esteem, were utterly impoverished and in danger of famine, as they had no money left with which to buy their customary provisions.

Speaking of the soldiers reminds me to add further details. The Roman emperors hitherto had stationed large armies on all frontiers of the State to protect its boundaries; and particularly in the East, to repel incursions of the Persians and Saracens. These border troops Justinian used so ill and meanly from the start that their pay became four or five years overdue; and when peace was declared between the Romans and Persians, these poor men, instead of sharing in the fruits of peace, were forced to contribute to the public treasury whatever was owed them; after which they were summarily discharged from the army. Thereafter the boundaries of the Roman Empire were unguarded, and the soldiers were left suddenly on the hands of charity.

Another corps of not less than three thousand, five hundred other soldiers, originally mustered for the palace guard, and called the Scholars, had always received higher pay from the public treasury than the rest of the army. Originally they were chosen to this preferred company by special merit, from the Armenians; but from the time when Zeno became Emperor, it was possible for anyone, no matter how poor or cowardly a soldier, to wear this uniform. Now when Justin came to the throne, this Justinian distributed the honor among a large number upon their paying him a considerable price for it. And when he saw there was no further possible vacancy, he enrolled two thousand more, whom he called Supernumeraries. When he himself took over the throne, he immediately disbanded the Supernumeraries, without giving them back any of the money they had paid him.

This, however, is what he schemed with reference to the Student Corps. Whenever an army was about to be sent against Libya, Italy, or the Persians, he ordered them to pack for service with the regulars, though he knew well they were utterly unfit for the campaign. And they, trembling at the possibility of active service, surrendered their pay for the period of the war. The Students had this unpleasant experience more than once. Also Peter, during all the time he was Master of Offices, worried them daily with unheard-of thefts.

For he was a gentle seeming and unassuming man, but the biggest thief alive, and simply bursting with sordid meanness. It was this Peter whom I mentioned before as responsible for the murder of Amasalontha, Theodoric's daughter.

There were also others in the palace guard of much higher rank; and the more they paid into the treasury for their commissions, the higher was their military rating. These were called Domestics and Protectors, and had always been exempt from active service. Only as a matter of form they were listed in the palace guard. Some of them were regularly stationed in Constantinople, others had always been assigned to Galatia or other provinces. Justinian scared these, too, in the same way, into forfeiting their pay to him.

Finally, it was the law that every five years the Emperor should give each soldier a bonus of a fixed sum in gold. And every five years commissioners had been sent over all the Roman Empire to give each soldier five gold staters. Not to comply with this custom was simply unthinkable. Yet from the time that this man managed the State, he never once did this, nor had any idea of doing it, though he reigned for thirty-two years: so that the very custom was finally forgotten by everyone.

### XXV. HOW HE ROBBED HIS OWN OFFICIALS

I will next describe another way in which he robbed his subjects. Those who serve the Emperor and the magistrates in Constantinople, either as guards or as secretaries or what not, are inscribed last in the list of officials. As time goes on, their rank advances as their superiors die or retire and they replace them, until they reach the topmost dignity. Those who attained this highest rank, according to the long-established rule, were paid more than one hundred gold centenaries a year, so as to have a competence for their old age, and that they might be able to discharge their many debts: which resulted in the affairs of state being competently and smoothly managed. But this Emperor deprived them of nearly all this money, to the great harm of these officials and everybody else. For poverty, attacking them first, soon spread to the others who formerly shared their solvency. And if one could calculate the sums of money thus lost during thirty-two years, he would know of how great a total they were thus deprived. This is how the tyrant used his military aides.

What he did to merchants and sailors, artisans and shop-keepers, and through them to everybody else, I will now relate. There are two straits on either side of Constantinople: one in the Hellespont between Sestos and Abydus, the other at the mouth of the Euxine Sea, where the Church of the Holy Mother is situated. Now in the Hellespontine strait there had been no customhouse, though an officer was stationed by the Emperor at Abydus, to see that no ship carrying a cargo of arms should pass to Constantinople without orders from the Emperor, and that no one should set sail from Constantinople without papers signed by the proper officials; for no ship was allowed to leave Constantinople without permission of the bureau of the Master of Offices. The toll exacted from the ship-owners, however, had been inconsequential. The officer stationed at the other strait received a regular salary from the Emperor, and his duty was exactly the same, to see that nothing was transported to the barbarians dwelling beyond the Euxine that was not permitted to be sent from Roman to hostile territory; but he was not allowed to collect any duties from navigators at this point.

But as soon as Justinian became Emperor, he stationed a customhouse at either strait, under two salaried officials, to whom he gave full power to collect as much money as they found possible. Eager to show their zeal, they made the mariners pay such tributes on everything as pirates might have exacted. And this was done at both straits.

At Constantinople, he concocted the following scheme. He appointed one of his intimates, a Syrian named Addeus, in charge of the port, with orders to collect duty from the ships anchoring there. And he, accordingly, never allowed any of the vessels putting in to Constantinople to leave until their owners either paid clearance fees or submitted to taking a cargo for Libya or Italy. Some of the shipowners, however, refused to submit to this compulsion, preferring to burn their boats rather than sail at such a price; and considered themselves lucky to escape with this sacrifice. Those who had to continue sailing in order to live, on the other hand, charged merchants three times the former rate for carrying their wares: so that the merchants had to recoup these losses by selling their stuff to individual purchasers at a correspondingly high price, with the result that the Romans nearly died of starvation.

This was the state of affairs throughout the Empire.

I must not omit, I suppose, mention of what the rulers did to the petty coinage. Formerly the money changers had customarily given two hundred and ten obols, or "folles," for one gold stater; but Justinian and Theodora, as a scheme for their private profit, ordered that only one hundred and eighty obols should be given for a stater. In this way they clipped off one sixth of each gold coin possessed by the people.

By licensing monopolies of nearly all kinds of wares, these rulers daily oppressed the purchasers; the sale of clothes was the only thing they left untouched, and even in this case they contrived the following scheme. Cloaks of silk had long been made in Berytus and

Tyre, in Phoenicia. Merchants who dwelt in these, and all the artisans and workers connected with the trade, had settled there in early times, and from these cities this trade had spread throughout the earth. But during the reign of Justinian, those in this business at Constantinople and in the other cities, raised the price of these garments: claiming that the price for such stuffs had been raised by the Persians, and that the import duties to Roman territory were also higher.

The Emperor, pretending to be incensed at this, proclaimed by edict that such clothing could not be sold for more than eight gold coins a pound; and the punishment for disobeying this law was the confiscation of the transgressor's property. This seemed to everybody impossible and futile. For it was not practicable for the merchants, who imported silk at a higher price, to sell it to their customers for less. Consequently they decided to stop dealing in it at all, and privately got rid of their present stock as best they could, selling it to such notables as took pleasure in throwing away their money for such finery, or thought they had to wear it.

The Empress, hearing what was going on through her whispering spies, without stopping to verify the rumor, immediately confiscated these persons' wares, fining them a centenary in addition. Now the imperial treasurer is supposed to be in charge of all matters connected with this trade. So when Peter Barsyames was given that office, they soon left it to him to do their unholy deeds. He ruled that all should obey the letter of the law, while he ordered the silk makers to work for himself. And this was no secret, for he sold colored silk in the Forum at six gold pieces an ounce, while

123

for the imperial dye, which is known as holovere, he charged more than twenty-four.

In this way he got much money for the Emperor and more, quietly, for himself; and the custom he started continues to this day, the treasurer being admittedly the sole silk merchant and controller of this trade.

The former dealers in silk in Constantinople and every other city, by sea and by land, were naturally heavily damaged. Almost the whole populace in the cities mentioned were suddenly made beggars. Artisans and mechanics were forced to struggle against famine, and many consequently left the country and fled to Persia. Only the imperial treasurer could transact this business, giving a share of the profits aforesaid to the Emperor, and himself taking most of them, fattening on the public calamity. And so much for that.

## XXVI. HOW HE SPOILED THE BEAUTY OF THE CITIES AND PLUNDERED THE POOR

How he ruined the beauty and appearance of Constantinople and every other city, we shall now see.

First he determined to debase the standing of the lawyers. He deprived them of all court fees, by which they had formerly lived in comfort and elegance; and in consequence they lost caste and significance. And after he had confiscated the estates of the Senators and other prosperous people, as has been related, in Constantinople and all over the Roman Empire, there was little use for lawyers anyway; men no longer had anything worth mentioning to go to court about. So of all the many noted advocates, only a few were left; and they were despised and reduced to penury, reaping nothing but insult from their work.

Furthermore, he caused physicians and teachers of the liberal arts to be deprived of the necessities of life. For he stopped all their living subsidies, which former emperors had paid men of these professions from the public treasury.

Also all of the taxes which the municipalities had devoted to public use or entertainments, he transferred arbitrarily to the imperial treasury. No consideration was now given to any physician or teacher; no one dared pay any attention to public buildings; there were no public lights in any city, nor any entertainments for the citizens. For the theaters, hippodromes, and circuses, in which his wife had been born, bred and educated, were all discontinued. Later he even stopped the public spectacles in Constantinople, to avoid spending the usual State money on them, by which an almost incalculable number of people had got their livelihood. On these, individually and collectively, ruin and desuetude descended, and as if some cataclysm had fallen on them from Heaven, their happiness was slain. And no other subject was spoken of among men, at home or in public or in the churches, than their calamities, their sufferings, and their overwhelming by the latest misfortune. Such was the state of affairs in the cities.

Of what is left to tell, this is worth mentioning. Each year two Roman consuls were appointed: one at Rome, the other at Constantinople. And whoever was called to this honor was expected to spend more than twenty gold centenaries on the public; some of which came from the Consul's private purse, but most was furnished by the Emperor. This money was given to those others whom I have mentioned, but mostly to the poor and those employed in the theater; all of which was to the good of the city. But from the time Justinian came to power, these distributions were not made at the customary time; for sometimes a Consul remained in office for year after year, till finally people wearied of hoping for a new one, even in their dreams. As a result, universal poverty was the case, since the usual annual relief was no longer afforded to subjects; and in every way all that they had was taken from them by their ruler.

Now I think I have shown sufficiently how this destroyer devoured all the public moneys and robbed each member of the Senate, publicly and privately, of all his estates; and how by bringing false charges he confiscated the properties of everybody else who was reputed to be wealthy, I imagine I have adequately told: as in the case of the soldiers, subordinate officers, and the palace guard; the farmers and landowners; those whose business is in words; merchants, shipowners and sailors; mechanics, artisans, and market dealers; those whose livelihood is in the theater; and indeed everyone else, who was affected in turn by the damage done to these. And now let us see what he did to those in need of alms: the poor, the beggars, and the diseased; for what he did to the priests will be described later.

First, as I have said, he took control of all the shops, licensed monopolies of all the wares most necessary to life, and exacted a price of more than triple their worth from the citizens. And other details of what he did I would not even attempt to catalogue in an endless book, since they were simply uncountable.

He put a bitter and perpetual tax on the sale of bread, which the day laborers, the poor and the infirm could not help buying. From this source he demanded three centenaries a year, with the result that the bakers filled their loaves with shells and dust; for the Emperor had no scruples against profiting meanly from even this unholy adulteration. Those in charge of the markets, turning this trick to their private gain, with ease became very wealthy and reduced the poor to an unexpected famine even in prosperous times; since it was not permitted to bring in grain from other places, but all were forced to eat bread purchased in the city.

One of the municipal aqueducts, which furnished not a small share of the city water, collapsed; but the rulers disregarded the matter and refused to repair it, though the constant crowds who had to use the wells were fairly stifling, and all the baths were shut down. On the other hand, he threw away great sums of money senselessly on buildings by the seashore and elsewhere, in all the suburbs, as if the palaces in which all the former emperors had been content to dwell were not enough for this pair. So it was not to save money, but to destroy his subjects, that he refused to rebuild the aqueduct; for no one in all history had ever been born among men more eager than Justinian to get hold of money, and then to throw it immediately away again. Through the two things left to them to drink and eat, water and bread, this Emperor injured those who were in the last extremes of poverty; making the one hard to procure at all, and the other too expensive to buy.

This he did not only to the poor in Constantinople, but to inhabitants elsewhere, as I shall now relate. When Theodoric captured Italy, he permitted the palace guard to remain in Rome, that some trace of the ancient State might be left; and he continued their daily pay. These soldiers were quite numerous, comprising the Silentiarii, the Domestics, and the Student Corps, who were soldiers only in name; their pay was just enough to live on; and Theodoric ordered that this should revert, on their deaths, to their children and families. Among the poor, who lived near the Church of St. Peter the Apostle, he distributed each year three thousand bushels of grain from the public granary; which they continued to receive until the arrival in Italy of Alexander the Scissors.

This man immediately decided to deprive them of all this. When Justinian, Emperor of the Romans, learned of this economy, he was greatly pleased, and favored Alexander more than ever. It was on his way here that Alexander treated the Greeks as follows. The fortress at Thermopylae had long been guarded by the neighboring farmers, who took turns watching the wall whenever an incursion of barbarians into the Peloponnese was anticipated.

But this Alexander, when he arrived there, claimed it was to the advantage of the Peloponnesians not to allow this pass to be kept by farmers. So he stationed two thousand soldiers there, to be paid not out of the imperial treasury, but by all the cities of Greece; and on this pretext, he diverted all their public and entertainment revenues to the general fund, saying that from it food would be bought for these soldiers. In consequence, after this, everywhere in Greece, including even Athens, no public buildings or any other benefit could be considered. But Justinian of course approved this action of the Scissors. And that is what happened here.

Then there is the matter of the poor in Alexandria. Among the lawyers there was one Hephaestus, who, on being made Governor of Alexandria, put a stop to civic sedition by intimidating the rioters, but reduced all the inhabitants to the utmost misery. For he immediately brought all the wares in the city under a monopoly, forbidding other merchants to sell anything, and himself became the only dealer and sole vendor of all wares: fixing prices as he pleased under his supreme power. By the consequent shortage in necessary provisions the city of Alexandria was greatly distressed, where formerly even the very poor had been able to live adequately; and the high price of bread pinched them most. For he alone bought up all the grain in Egypt, not allowing anyone else to purchase as much as a single bushel; and thus he controlled the supply and price of bread as he pleased. In this way he soon amassed unheard-of wealth, at the same time satisfying the greed of the Emperor. The people of Alexandria through fear of Hephaestus bore their suffering in silence; and the Emperor, awed by the abundance of money that continuously came to him from that quarter, was wonderfully delighted with his Governor.

This Hephaestus, planning to incur even greater favor of the Emperor, contrived the following additional scheme. When Diocletian became ruler of the Romans, he ordered a large quantity of grain to be given yearly to the poor in Alexandria. And the Alexandrians, distributing this among themselves at that time, had transmitted the right to receive this bounty to their descendants up to this time. But Hephaestus, depriving these needy ones of this charity, which amounted to two million bushels, diverted it to the imperial granary, and wrote to the Emperor that these men had been getting this dole unjustly and not in accordance with the interests of state. The Emperor, approving this action, was still fonder of him than before. But such Alexandrians whose hope of life had been in the distribution, in their present bitter distress felt the full benefit of his inhumanity.

## XXVII. HOW THE DEFENDER OF THE FAITH PROTECTED THE INTERESTS OF THE CHRISTIANS

The deeds of Justinian were such that all eternity would not be long enough in which to describe them adequately. So a few examples will have to suffice to illuminate his whole character to future generations: what a dissembler he was, how he disregarded God, the priests, the laws, and the people who showed themselves loyal to him. He had no shame at all, either when he brought destruction on the State or at any misdeed; he did not bother to try to excuse his actions, and his only care was how he might get sole possession of all the wealth of the world. To begin:

As bishop of Alexandria he appointed a man by the name of Paul. At this time one Rhodon, a Phoenician, was Governor of that city. Him he ordered to serve Paul with all zeal, and to allow none of his instructions to be unfulfilled. For thus he thought he could associate all the priests in Alexandria under the synod of Chalcedon.

Now there was a certain Arsenius, a native of Palestine, who had become one of the most useful intimates of the Empress Theodora, and consequently after acquiring great power and wealth, had been raised to senatorial rank, though he was a disgusting fellow. He was a Samaritan, but so as not to lose his official rank and power, became a nominal Christian; while his father and brother, encouraged by his authority, continued in their ancestral faith in Scythopolis, where, with his consent, they persecuted the Christians intolerably. As a result of this, the citizens revolted and put them both to a most shameful death. Many later troubles afflicted the people of Palestine because of this. At the time, however, neither Justinian nor the Empress did anything to punish Arsenius, though he was principally responsible for the whole trouble. They merely forbade him entrance to the palace, to get rid of the crowds of Christians complaining against him.

This Arsenius, thinking to please the Emperor, soon after went to Alexandria with Paul, to assist him generally and in special to help him get the good will of the Alexandrians. For during the time he had been barred from the palace, he affirmed he had become learned in all the Christian doctrines. This displeased Theodora, for she pretended to disagree with the Emperor in religious matters, as I have told before.

As soon as they arrived in Alexandria, Paul handed over a deacon by the name of Psoes to Rhodon to be put to death, on the charge that this man alone stood in the way of the accomplishment of the Emperor's wishes. And following instructions in letters from the Emperor, which came frequently and cogently, Rhodon ordered the man to be scourged; after which, while he was being racked by the torture, he up and died.

When news of this reached the Emperor, at the Empress's instigation he expressed horror at what had been done by Paul, Rhodon and Arsenius: as if he had forgotten his own instructions to these men. He now appointed Liberius, a patrician from Rome, Governor of Alexandria, and sent certain priests of good reputation to Alexandria, to investigate the matter; among these were the Archdeacon of Rome, Pelagius, who was commissioned by Pope Vigilius to act as his legate.

Paul, convicted of the murder, was removed from the bishopric; Rhodon, who fled to Constantinople, was beheaded by the Emperor and his estates confiscated, although the man produced thirteen letters which the Emperor had written him, insisting and commanding him to serve Paul in everything and never to oppose him, so that he could fulfill his every wish in religious matters. Liberius, at Theodora's order, crucified Arsenius, and the Emperor confiscated his property, though he had no charge to bring against him except that he had been intimate with Paul. Now whether his actions in this matter were just or otherwise, I cannot say; but I shall soon show why I have described the affair.

Some time later, Paul came to Constantinople and offered the Emperor seven gold centenaries if he would reinstate him in the holy office from which, he claimed, he had been illegally removed. Justinian genially took the money, treated the man with great respect, and agreed to make him Bishop of Alexandria again very soon, though another now held the office; as if he did not know that he himself had put to death Paul's friends and helpers, and had confiscated their estates.

So the Augustus zealously extended every effort to arrange this matter, and Paul was generally expected to regain his bishopric one way or another. But Vigilius, who was in the capital at the time, decided not to yield to the Emperor's command in such a case; and he said he could not annul a decision which Pelagius had given as his legate. And the Emperor, whose only idea was to get the money, dismissed the matter.

Here is another similar case. There was a certain Faustin, born in Palestine, and of an old Samaritan family, who accepted a nominal Christianity when the law constrained him. This Faustin became a Senator and a Governor of his province; and when his term of office expired a little later, he came to Constantinople, where he was denounced by certain priests as having favored the Samaritans and impiously persecuted the Christians in Palestine. Justinian appeared to be very angry and outraged that during his rule over the Romans, anybody could have insulted the name of Christ.

So the Senate investigated the affair and by the will of the Emperor, punished Faustin with exile. But the Emperor, after getting from him the money he wanted, straightway annulled the decree. And Faustin, restored to his former rank, and the Emperor's friendship, was made Count of the imperial domains in Palestine and Phoenicia, where he fearlessly did as much harm as he wanted. Now in what way Justinian protected the true interests of the Christians may clearly be seen in these instances, few of them as I have had time to give.

## XXVIII. HIS VIOLATION OF THE LAWS OF THE ROMANS, AND HOW JEWS WERE FINED FOR EATING LAMB

How he unhesitatingly abolished laws when money was in question will now be shown in a few words. There was one Priscus in the City of Emesa, who was a skilful forger of others' handwriting, and a rare artist in such crime. It happened that the church of Emesa had a long time before inherited the property of a distinguished patrician named Mammian, of illustrious family and of great wealth. During Justinian's reign, Priscus inventoried all the families of the mentioned city, so as to find which were adequately rich to be worth plundering, and after he investigated their family history, and found ancient letters in their ancestors' handwriting, he forged documents purporting to be their agreements to pay to Mammian large sums of money which were supposed to have been left with them by him as a deposit.

The amount of money mentioned as an obligation in these forgeries was not less than one hundred gold centenaries. He also imitated very craftily the writing of a certain notary public whose office was in the Forum during Mammian's lifetime: a man of high reputation for truth and every other virtue, who used to draw up all the citizens' documents, fixing them with his own seal. To those who were in charge of ecclesiastical affairs at Emesa he gave these documents, after they agreed that he would get a share of the money to be obtained from the matter.

But since there was a statute of limitations barring action after thirty years, except in mortgages and certain other matters, where the limit was forty years, they formed the following plan. Going to Constantinople and offering the Emperor large sums of money, they begged him to join in accomplishing the destruction of their innocent fellow citizens. He took the money, and without scruple published a new law, to the effect that the statute of limitations did not apply to the church, but claims connected with that institution might be brought at any time within a hundred years. And this was now the law not only in Emesa, but throughout the whole Roman Empire.

To enforce his decree he sent to Emesa one Longinus, a man of deeds and of great bodily strength, who later was Prefect of Constantinople. And those in charge of church affairs there immediately brought suit for two centenaries against some of the citizens whose ancestors were mentioned in the forgeries; and soon obtained judgment against these men, who had no defence owing to the great lapse of time and their ignorance of the facts. And all the other citizens were greatly grieved over this, and incensed against the accusers; the most reputable men of Emesa being the most perturbed.

Just as this evil was now progressing against the majority of the citizens, Providence intervened in the following way. Longinus ordered Priscus, the inventor of the mischievous trick, to bring him all the documents in the case; and when he objected, slapped him with all his might. Priscus, unable to bear the shock of a blow from a strong man, fell on his back, now trembling and shaking with fear; and supposing that Longinus had discovered him and that the whole deceit had been brought to light, stopped bringing suits.

As if it were not enough to do away with the laws of the Romans daily, the Emperor also exerted himself to destroy the traditions of the Jews. For whenever in their calendar Passover came before the Christian Easter, he forbade the Jews to celebrate it on their proper day, to make then any sacrifices to God or perform any of their customs. Many of them were heavily fined by the magistrates for eating lamb at such times, as if this were against the laws of the State.

Knowing countless other such acts of Justinian, I cannot include them, since the end of this book draws near. In any case, what I have told will be enough to show the nature of the man.

I will now show what a liar and hypocrite he was. This
Liberius, whom I recently mentioned, he removed from
office and in his stead appointed John, an Egyptian,
surnamed Laxarion. When Pelagius, a particular friend
of Liberius's, heard of this, he asked the Emperor if the
report about Laxarion's appointment were true. And
he immediately denied it, assuring him he had done
nothing of the sort; and gave him a letter to take to
Liberius charging him to stick tight to his office and
give it over to nobody, as he, Justinian, had not the
slightest idea of removing him from it at this time.

Now John had an uncle in Constantinople named
Eudemon, of consular rank and great wealth, who was
at the time Count of the imperial estates. This Eudemon, when he heard the rumor, also went to the Emperor to inquire if the office were really going to his
nephew. And Justinian, in contradiction of what he
had written to Liberius, now wrote a document to
John, telling him to take over the office by all means,
as his intentions were unchanged. John, trusting in this
instruction, ordered Liberius to retire from his office
as he had been officially removed. But Liberius, with
equal confidence, of course, in the letter he had had
from the Emperor, refused. So John went after Liberius
with an armed guard, and Liberius with his own

guard defended himself. During the fight many were killed, including John himself, the new Governor.

Now at Eudemon's instigation, Liberius was summoned to Constantinople; the Senate investigated the affair, and acquitted Liberius, since what he did had been in self-defense. The Emperor, however, did not let him off until he had privately paid him a fine. This shows Justinian's love of truth and how he kept his word.

It might not be out of the way for me to tell a sequel of this incident. This Eudemon died a little later, leaving many relatives but no will of any kind. About the same time the chief eunuch of the palace, Euphrates, was released from life, leaving a nephew but no will disposing of his considerable property. The Emperor seized both estates, making himself the arbitrary heir, and did not give as much as a three-obol piece to the legal inheritors. Such was the respect for law and the kinsmen of his friends that this Emperor had. So, also, he seized the estate of Ireneus, who had died some time before, without any proper claim to it of any kind.

Another thing that happened at this time I must also not fail to tell. One Anatolius was foremost in the Senate of Ascalon. His daughter was married to a citizen of Caesarea by the name of Mamilian, of illustrious family. This girl was Anatolius's legal heir, since she was his only child. Now there was an ancient law that when a Senator of any of the cities departed this world, leaving no male issue, one fourth of his estate should go to the Senate of his city, and all the rest to his heirs. Here again the tyrant had showed his true character. He made a new law reversing the rule, decreeing that when a Senator died without male issue, his heirs should get one fourth of his estate, and all the rest should go to the imperial treasury and the local Senate. Never in the memory of man had the treasury or the Emperor shared the estate of a Senator.

While this new law was in force, Anatolius reached the final day of his life. His daughter was about to divide her inheritance with the treasury and the city Senate according to the law, when she received letters from both the Emperor and the Ascalon Senate, dismissing all their claims to the property, on the ground they had already all that was properly their just due.

Later Mamilian also died, Anatolius's son-in-law, leaving one daughter, who of course inherited his estate. While her mother was still living, this daughter too died, after marrying a man of distinction by whom she had no children, male or female. Justinian immediately seized the whole estate, on the remarkable ground that it would be an unholy thing for the daughter of Anatolius, an old woman, to become rich on the property of both her father and her husband. But that the woman might not be reduced to beggary, he ordered her to be given one gold stater a day so long as she lived: writing in the decree by which he robbed her of these properties that he was granting her this stater for the sake of religion, "for it is my custom to do what is holy and pious."

This will have to suffice, in order that my book may not be overfilled with such anecdotes; and indeed, no one man could recall everything he did.

I will show how he cared nothing for even the Blues, who were devoted to him, when money was at stake.

There was a Cilician named Malthanes, son-in-law of that Leo who was, as I have said, a Referendar. Justinian sent this Malthanes to restore order among the Cilicians. On this pretext Malthanes inflicted intolerable sufferings on most of his fellow citizens, and robbed them of their money, some of which he sent to the tyrant, enriching himself unjustly with the rest.

Now some bore their sufferings in silence; but those of the inhabitants of Tarsus who were Blues, trusting in the favor of the Empress, assembled in their Forum to insult Malthanes, who was not present. When Malthanes heard of this, he assembled a body of soldiers and arrived in Tarsus by night; and sending his soldiers into the private houses, ordered them to put the inhabitants to death. Thinking this was an invasion by an enemy, the Blues defended themselves. And among other evils that took place in the darkness, it happened that Damian, a Senator, was killed by an arrow wound.

This Damian was president of the local Blues; and when the news came to Constantinople, the indignant Blues there made a great uproar throughout the city, and gathered in crowds to complain violently to the Emperor, while they uttered terrible threats against Leo and Malthanes. The Emperor pretended to be no less outraged at the affair, and immediately wrote to order an investigation and punishment of Malthanes by his citizens. But Leo gave him a large sum of money, so he stopped inquiry and his interest in the Blues.

With the affair thus unsettled, the Emperor received Malthanes at Constantinople with all favor and esteem. As he was leaving the imperial presence, the Blues, who had been on the lookout for him, attacked him in the very palace and would have killed him, if some of their party, who had been bribed by Leo, had not stopped them. Who would not call that state most miserable, in which the Emperor accepts bribes to leave an inquiry unfinished, and in which factionists, while the Emperor is in the palace, dare to mutiny against one of their own magistrates and lift violent hands against him? However, no punishment for this was ever brought on either Malthanes or those who attacked him. And from this alone, if you pleased, you could prove the character of Justinian.

## XXX. FURTHER INNOVATIONS OF JUSTINIAN AND THEODORA, AND A CONCLUSION

How much he cared for the interests of the State may be seen by what he did to the public couriers and the spies. For the preceding Roman emperors, so that they might most quickly and easily have news of enemy invasions into any province, of sedition in the cities or any other unexpected trouble, of the actions of the governors and everyone else everywhere in the Roman Empire, and also so that those bringing in the annual taxes might be kept from delay and danger, had established a system of public couriers everywhere in the following manner.

As a day's journey for an active man, they decided on eight stages in some places, in others less, but hardly ever less than five. Forty horses were kept for each stage, and grooms in proportion to the number of horses. By frequent relays of the best mounts, couriers were thus able to ride as long a distance in one day as would ordinarily require ten, and bring with them the news required. Also the landowners in these provinces, especially those whose estates were in the interior, were greatly benefited by the system, as they sold at a high price to the government each year their surplus harvests to feed the horses and the grooms. And accordingly the State received the due tribute from each of these, immediately reimbursing them for furnishing it: and this was to the advantage of the whole State. Now this is how things were formerly done.

But this tyrant first suppressed the post from Chalcedon to Dacibiza, and then compelled the couriers to go from Constantinople to Helenopolis, however little they liked it, by sea. Faring in small boats, such as were usually used for crossing the strait, they were in serious peril if a storm came up. For because speed was demanded of them, they could not wait for calm weather. In the case of the road to Persia, he permitted the former system to remain; but everywhere else in the East, as far as Egypt, he reduced the number of stages making a day's journey to one, and provided, instead of horses, a few asses. Consequently news of what happened in each province was brought with great difficulty, too late to be of any use and long after the event, and the farm owners got no benefit of their crops which either rotted or lay idle.

The spies were organized as follows. Many men were formerly supported by the treasury, who visited the enemy, especially the Persian court, to find out exactly what was going on; on their return to Roman territory, they were able to report to the Emperors the secrets of the enemy. And the Romans, being warned, were on guard and could not be taken by surprise. This system was also a long-established custom with the Medes; and Chosroes, they say, increased the pay of his spies, and benefited by the precaution. But Justinian did away with the practice of hiring Roman spies, and in consequence lost much territory to the enemy, including Lazica, which was taken because the Romans had no information as to where the Persian King was with his army.

The State had also always kept a large number of camels, which carried all the baggage when the Roman army marched against the foe. Thus the peasants did not have to carry burdens, and the soldiers lacked no necessity. But Justinian did away with almost all of these animals. Consequently when the Roman army now marches against the enemy, it is impossible for it to be supplied with what it needs. Such was the zeal he displayed for the interests of the State.

There is nothing like mentioning one of his ridiculous acts. Among the lawyers at Caesarea was one Evangelius, a man of no mean distinction, who, favored by the winds of Fate, became the master of much money and much land. Eventually he bought a village on the seacoast, named Porphyreon, for three gold centenaries. Learning of this, Justinian immediately took the place from him, giving him back only a small fraction of the price he had paid, and uttered the remark that it would never do for Evangelius, a mere lawyer, to be the lord of such a village. Well, we must stop somewhere when we begin to recall all these stories.

This, however, is worth telling among the innovations of Justinian and Theodora. Formerly, when the Senate approached the Emperor, it paid homage in the following manner. Every patrician kissed him on the right breast; the Emperor kissed the patrician on the head, and he was dismissed. Then the rest bent their right knee to the Emperor and withdrew. It was not customary to pay homage to the Queen.

But those who were admitted to the presence of Justinian and Theodora, whether they were patricians or otherwise, fell on their faces on the floor, stretching their hands and feet out wide, kissed first one foot and then the other of the Augustus, and then retired. Nor did Theodora refuse this honor; and she even received the ambassadors of the Persians and other barbarians and gave them presents, as if she were in command of the Roman Empire: a thing that had never happened in all previous time.

And formerly intimates of the Emperor called him Emperor and the Empress, Empress; and the other officials according to the title of their rank. But if anybody addressed either of these two as Emperor or Empress without adding "Your Majesty" or "Your Highness," or forgot to call himself their slave, he was considered either ignorant or insolent, and was dismissed in disgrace as if he had done some awful crime or committed an unpardonable sin.

And before, only a few were sometimes admitted to

the palace; but from the time when these two came to power, the magistrates and everybody else had no trouble in fairly living in the palace. This was because the magistrates of old had administered justice and the laws according to their conscience, and made their decisions while in their own offices, while their subjects, neither seeing nor hearing any injustice, of course had little cause to trouble the Emperor. But these two, taking control of everything to the misfortune of their subjects, forced everyone to come to them and beg like slaves. And almost any day one could see the law courts nearly deserted, while in the hall of the Emperor there was a jostling and pushing crowd that resembled nothing so much as a mob of slaves.

Those who were supposed to be in the imperial favor would stand there all day and most of the night, sleepless and foodless, until they were exhausted; and this is what their presumed good fortune got them. And those who were free of all this sort of thing, asked each other what would become of the prosperity of the Romans. For some were sure it was already in the hands of the barbarians, and others said the Emperor had hidden it away in his various dwelling places. But only when Justinian, be he man or King of the Devils, shall have departed this life, shall they who then happen to survive him, discover the truth.